blished by AvidBook publishing Agency

CODE AS LEGACY

Writing Systems Th
Outlive Their Creat

Francis Odinaka

Table Of Contents

Preface

When humanity first began writing, clay tablets carried the imprints of symbols that spoke to those who would come centuries later. The marks were not meant for immediate consumption alone. They were meant to carry forward memory, knowledge, and instruction. In the same way, the modern age has created a new form of writing, one that does not dwell on stone or papyrus but resides in the silent architecture of digital systems. This writing is code. Unlike ancient writing systems, which required interpretation by scholars and translations across generations, code contains both instruction and execution. It is a living form of writing, one that commands machines and also informs human imagination. This book is born from a recognition that code is not simply functional. Code is legacy. It carries forward the vision of its author, extending beyond the hands that typed it into the minds and futures of those who will maintain it, inherit it, and reshape it.

Foreword

The world we live in has been architected by invisible authors. When you pick up a smartphone, open an application, browse the web, or even withdraw money from an ATM, you are interacting with systems that were designed by individuals you will never meet. Many of these individuals are no longer alive. Yet their work persists, shaping the rhythms of commerce, communication, and culture. Few realize that behind every click and every process lies code written years, sometimes decades ago. Code is not simply instruction. It is inheritance. As someone who has worked in technology for decades, I have seen the truth of this reality unfold in countless ways.

Introduction

The first time I saw code that outlived its author, I was struck by the quiet power of continuity. It was not in a celebrated library or a famous system. It was in a small script buried deep inside the infrastructure of a company. The script had been written years earlier by a developer who had long since left. The company no longer remembered the author's name. Yet every morning, that script executed faithfully, processing data that was essential for daily operations. The script had become invisible, taken for granted, assumed to be eternal. It had outlived not only the tenure of its author but also the entire generation of employees who once knew its origin. That was when I realized that code was not simply temporary. It was legacy. We live in a paradox. Technology changes faster than any other domain of human activity. Languages emerge and fade. Frameworks rise and collapse. Systems are replaced in months where once they lasted decades. And yet, within this rapid churn, certain codes and systems endure. Some endure by design, others by accident. Some endure because they are too costly to replace, others because they are too well written to abandon. The reality is that much of our world now runs on code written by people who are gone. This book begins with that recognition. Code is not just execution. It is continuation. It is the means by which we communicate with the future. It is the most significant cultural act of our age, because unlike literature or art, it does not merely express. It governs. .When we talk about legacy in human life, we often think of inheritance, of family, of reputation, of cultural contributions. Rarely do we think of code. Yet in truth, code is now one of the greatest inheritances we pass on. Every programmer writes something that will either dissolve into irrelevance or persist into the future. Every developer has the potential to shape systems that others will depend on long after they themselves are gone. The more deeply we examine code, the more we see that it is not simply a mechanism for instructing machines. It is a cultural artifact. It is the crystallization of thought in a form that can both be read and executed. Unlike literature, which must always be interpreted by the human mind, code carries within it the extraordinary ability to act. It does not wait for interpretation. It does not rely on opinion. When written correctly, it executes faithfully across years, across hardware, across systems, often unchanged. This dual nature of code, at once text and action, makes it one of the most unique creations in human history.

To understand the significance of code as legacy, we must remember that human civilizations have always depended on forms of writing to carry continuity forward. The Sumerians carved records into stone tablets not because they loved stone, but because stone would endure. Monks in medieval Europe painstakingly copied manuscripts, knowing that their work was the bridge between generations. Nations kept archives, scholars wrote treatises, artists created symbols, all in the hope that their efforts would outlast the moment in which they lived. Code participates in this same tradition. It is humanity's most modern script, one that bridges not only time but also the boundary between thought and action. Yet there is a crucial difference between traditional writing and code. Traditional writing depends on cultural interpretation, context, and translation. The meaning of a poem shifts depending on the reader, the age, and the cultural lens. Code, however, though it requires context to understand, possesses an unyielding clarity when executed. A loop remains a loop. A function remains a function. An algorithm continues to sort numbers in the same sequence, whether executed today or thirty years from now. Of course, environments change, and dependencies evolve, but the underlying logic of code carries an endurance that few other human writings can claim.

When we say that code outlives its creator, we are making both a technical and philosophical claim. Technically, countless systems prove this truth every day. Banks continue to run COBOL programs written before many of their current employees were born. Aviation systems operate with code that was first written decades ago, still reliable enough to carry human lives across the skies. Medical equipment, satellites, industrial machines, and even modern websites often contain fragments of code that predate the current era. Philosophically, the endurance of code reflects something profound about human intention. To write code is to create not only for now, but for an unknown future. The programmer rarely knows who will use, modify, or inherit their code. Yet the decisions they make will shape experiences, opportunities, and limitations for generations to come.

The irony of code is that it is at once ephemeral and eternal. Ephemeral, because frameworks change, languages evolve, and what is fashionable today may be forgotten tomorrow. Eternal, because certain logics, algorithms, and systems continue unchanged, silently embedded in the infrastructure of daily life. This paradox demands humility. It reminds us that while we chase novelty, we are also building continuity. The most ordinary script written today may become the backbone of something extraordinary tomorrow. Another truth lies at the heart of code as legacy. Code does not endure by accident alone. It endures because of decisions. It endures when it is written with clarity, when it is structured for maintainability, when it carries documentation that speaks across time. It endures when the author understands that future developers, unknown and unnamed, will one day encounter this code and will either bless the author for their foresight or curse them for their neglect. Every programmer has encountered code that felt like an unsolvable riddle, written in obscurity, with no guidance, no clarity, no sense of inheritance. In those moments, we experience the darker side of legacy. Neglect can live as long as brilliance.

This book argues that coding must be seen as authorship. Every author, whether writing literature, philosophy, or technical text, knows that words may travel beyond their immediate audience. In the same way, programmers must recognize that every function, every class, every system may travel beyond their immediate team. Authorship is not only about expression. It is about responsibility. It is about the recognition that what you release into the world may shape more lives than you can imagine.

Consider the invisible presence of legacy in your own daily life. When you log into a website, unseen code authenticates your identity. When you send a message, invisible protocols deliver it across the globe. When you pay a bill, lines written by programmers decades ago process that transaction. These are not temporary conveniences. They are the bones of digital civilization. And those bones were shaped by people who, at the time, likely thought they were solving a small problem. They did not know they were shaping the infrastructure of a world. The introduction to this book must then serve as both mirror and window. It is a mirror because it reflects back to every programmer the truth of their authorship, whether they have acknowledged it or not. It is a window because it opens into a larger vision, showing that code is not simply about technology but about human continuity. The challenge I lay before you as a reader is to see coding not as a fleeting task, but as a practice of legacy-building. Every time you open an editor, you are writing into the future. Every time you commit to a repository, you are leaving behind a mark that someone else may inherit. Every time you name a variable, you are speaking to another human being who will one day try to understand your intention. This is not a burden, though it is heavy. It is a privilege. To write code is to participate in one of the most significant acts of authorship humanity has ever created.

As you continue into the following chapters, you will see this truth unfold in greater detail. You will encounter stories of enduring systems. You will study principles of clarity and adaptability. You will explore the ethics of authorship in code. And you will be challenged to treat your work as part of a larger continuum, not a disposable task. This book does not seek to burden you with impossible perfection. It seeks to inspire you with responsibility. It seeks to remind you that the very act of writing code is an act of planting seeds, some of which may grow into forests that shelter lives far beyond your own.

Code is not merely technical. Code is cultural. Code is not merely instruction. Code is inheritance. Code is not merely present. Code is future. And the future, as it turns out, is always watching the past, always building upon it, always carrying it forward. To recognize this truth is to elevate programming from craft to authorship, from task to legacy.

Chapter One

Code as the New Language of Civilization

When human civilization first began to leave marks that would last beyond the voice, it was not because of necessity alone, but because of the recognition that memory needed vessels. The inscriptions on stone tablets, the hieroglyphics carved into monuments, the cuneiform etched into clay, all served as bridges from one generation to the next. Those inscriptions were not only symbolic; they were practical. They held laws, records, stories, and contracts. They allowed society to carry itself forward with continuity. In the same way, the modern world has birthed a new kind of inscription, one not etched on stone but encoded in the logic of machines. That inscription is code, and it has become the new universal language of civilization. Code differs from ancient languages in a fundamental way. While traditional language carries meaning through interpretation, code carries meaning through execution. A poem requires the reader to imagine, to decode its imagery, to feel its weight. A line of code requires the machine to act, to follow its logic, to produce outcome. This duality between traditional language and code is what gives coding its extraordinary position in human history. It is not merely communication; it is command. It is not only expression; it is execution. To treat it lightly is to misunderstand its power.

When we speak of code as the new language of civilization, we are pointing to the fact that code has become the unseen infrastructure of daily life. The global economy rests upon algorithms. Financial systems, transportation systems, communication systems, healthcare systems, and even governance are increasingly mediated by the invisible language of code. To live in the twenty-first century is to live in a society orchestrated not by the direct will of rulers or priests, but by the silent, continuous operation of software. In a sense, we are governed not only by laws written in parliaments, but also by laws written in programming languages. This raises profound implications for how we understand authorship. In previous civilizations, those who wrote scripture or philosophy or legal codes were seen as guardians of continuity. Their words mattered because their words directed human behavior. Today, those who write code carry a similar responsibility. Their lines of instruction may shape the behavior of millions without their names ever being known. Code has given rise to an anonymous form of authorship, one in which the writer may be forgotten, but the writing persists with astonishing authority. If code is language, then we must ask what makes a language endure. Latin endured because it became the foundation for education, law, and science for centuries. Arabic endured because it was tied to scholarship and faith across vast regions. Chinese script endured because it carried cultural continuity across dynasties. Code will endure because it is now tied to the functioning of society itself. Yet not all code will endure equally. Just as some languages disappeared while others persisted, so too will some systems vanish while others remain.

The endurance of code depends on clarity, adaptability, and relevance. A well-structured algorithm, like a well-constructed sentence, can travel across time with minimal decay. A chaotic function, like a poorly written manuscript, will soon collapse under the weight of confusion. Programmers, therefore, stand in the same place as ancient scribes. They must decide whether their work will be an enduring inscription or a forgotten note. This is the heart of the matter: coding is not only about solving problems; it is about writing for permanence. What makes code even more significant than traditional language is that its endurance does not depend on interpretation alone. While future readers may reinterpret Shakespeare, Dante, or Confucius in infinite ways, future systems will execute C, Java, or Python in precisely the same way, assuming the environment remains intact. This gives code a kind of reliability that no other human language can claim. It is, in a sense, the most faithful language ever invented. And yet, the paradox is that faithfulness does not guarantee understanding. Future programmers may execute code without ever grasping the intentions behind it. They may inherit systems without understanding the vision of those who wrote them. This is why documentation, clarity, and humility are essential. Without them, the inheritance becomes a curse. With them, the inheritance becomes a blessing. The language of code, like all languages, must be not only executable but also readable. The recognition of code as the new language of civilization should change how we view our work. It should push us to ask not only whether our code functions, but also whether it communicates, whether it endures, whether it carries forward meaning across time. Because when civilizations are studied centuries from now, it will not only be our literature or our monuments that tell our story. It will be our code. It will be the invisible instructions that govern how billions of lives interacted, transacted, and connected. In this sense, to write code is to write civilization itself.

The Invisible Architects of the Digital World

Civilizations have always been built by architects whose names were forgotten, even as their structures endured. The builders of the pyramids, the engineers of Roman aqueducts, the craftsmen of medieval cathedrals, all labored with the knowledge that their contributions might outlast them. They did not always seek fame, but they understood permanence. In the digital age, the new architects are programmers. Yet unlike the stone and steel of old, their work is invisible. It lives not in monuments but in machines, not in bricks but in logic, not in walls but in networks. They are the invisible architects of the digital world. The irony of this invisibility is that it often blinds us to the magnitude of their contribution. Few people walking through a city think about the structural engineers who designed the bridges, yet they trust those bridges with their lives. In the same way, few people sending an email, paying a bill, or streaming a video think about the programmer who wrote the code that makes it possible. Yet every moment of trust in the digital age rests upon the unseen labor of coders. To call programmers invisible architects is not only metaphor but truth. They are designing the skeleton of the modern world. And like architects, they face choices. An architect can build with cheap materials and poor design, creating a structure that will crumble within decades. Or they can build with foresight, creating something that will stand for centuries. In the same way, a programmer can build a quick fix that collapses under future strain, or they can build a system that remains functional, adaptable, and enduring. The invisibility of programmers raises both challenge and opportunity. The challenge is that their responsibility is often unrecognized. Decisions that will affect millions are made quietly, without ceremony, without recognition. The opportunity is that this invisibility allows for humility. It allows for the recognition that the work is not about personal glory, but about building structures that others will inherit. This humility is at the core of legacy. When we examine enduring systems, we see the fingerprints of invisible architects everywhere. We see it in the Unix operating system, which continues to form the foundation of countless technologies decades after its birth. We see it in programming languages like C, still shaping software across industries. We see it in protocols like TCP/IP, still governing the flow of data across the globe. These were not accidents. They were the work of architects who built with clarity, simplicity, and adaptability. They built not for the applause of the present, but for the endurance of the future. The lesson is clear. To code is to build architecture. It is to build invisible structures that others will trust, depend upon, and inhabit. The question is whether those structures will endure or collapse. Every programmer is an architect, whether they admit it or not. Every line of code is a brick, every function a wall, every system a building. The digital world is a city built of logic, and its architects are the programmers who write unseen.

The invisibility of programmers should not diminish their importance. Rather, it should deepen their sense of responsibility. When you are unseen, your work is judged not by your reputation, but by its endurance. When your name is forgotten, your code remains as the only testimony of your labor. That is the ultimate test of authorship. Not whether people remember you, but whether what you wrote continues to matter long after you are gone.

Legacy as Responsibility and Burden

The word legacy carries both hope and warning. It speaks about the possibility of endurance, but also about the inevitability of inheritance. To leave behind a legacy is not only to leave behind brilliance, but also to leave behind burdens. In the world of code, this truth is unavoidable. Every programmer leaves behind systems that someone else will one day inherit. The question is whether that inheritance will be a gift or a curse. When legacy is treated as responsibility, programmers write with the awareness that others will depend upon their work. They document clearly. They design modularly. They test thoroughly. They think not only of the immediate task but of the future reader, the future maintainer, the future user. They know that code is not only a tool for today but an inheritance for tomorrow. When legacy is neglected, the result is code that becomes a nightmare for future generations. Every developer has experienced the frustration of dealing with what is often called legacy code, code that is difficult to understand, poorly documented, and resistant to change. But the problem is not the age of the code. The problem is the neglect of responsibility at the moment of authorship. Code becomes a curse when its writer fails to imagine the future. This dual nature of legacy is what makes it both powerful and heavy. It reminds us that our work will outlive us, whether we intend it or not. It reminds us that every decision we make today may shape the experience of someone we will never meet. It reminds us that code is to take part in a chain of continuity that stretches across time. The burden of legacy can feel overwhelming. Programmers often work under pressure, driven by deadlines, constrained by resources. To think of the future while solving the present may feel impossible. Yet it is precisely in these moments that legacy must be remembered. Because even in haste, decisions shape outcomes. Even under pressure, structures are built. Even in neglect, inheritance is created.

The responsibility of legacy does not mean perfection. No code will be flawless. No system will be eternal. But responsibility means care. It means humility. It means remembering that what we create is not ours alone. It belongs to the future.

Legacy, then, is not only about what we build, but about how we build it. It is about whether we treat our work as disposable or as enduring. It is about whether we see ourselves as temporary problem-solvers or as authors of continuity. It is about whether we recognize that in every line we write, we are speaking not only to machines, but to generations of human beings who will inherit our choices.

This is the heart of code as legacy. It is the recognition that our work does not end with execution. It continues with inheritance. It continues with responsibility. It continues with the burden and blessing of knowing that what we build today may still govern lives tomorrow.

Chapter Two

The Language of Systems and the Weight of Inheritance

When a developer writes code, what emerges is more than a sequence of instructions processed by machines. It is a language that is simultaneously precise and interpretive, rigid yet fluid, structured yet expressive. Unlike casual conversation, code does not fade once spoken. It becomes a permanent architecture, a bridge between human logic and mechanical execution. In this sense, every system is both a linguistic artifact and a structural legacy. The inheritance of that system, by future maintainers and users, carries weight far beyond what the original author might have intended. To fully appreciate this inheritance, one must see code not as ephemeral problem-solving but as a lasting framework that future generations will be forced to interpret, extend, and sometimes endure. The act of writing code can often feel immediate. A problem exists in the present moment, a developer crafts a solution, and the software executes to fulfill the intended function. But beneath this immediacy lies a deeper permanence. Systems written decades ago continue to govern essential parts of society. Banks still depend on COBOL programs written in the mid-twentieth century. Transportation infrastructure is managed by code that predates many of the engineers currently working on it. Healthcare systems rely on legacy applications that outlive their original creators. This permanence transforms coding from a short-term technical act into a long-term cultural contribution. The language chosen, the architecture designed, and the clarity of structure embedded within it all shape how inheritance will unfold. Consider the concept of language itself. Human languages evolve, adapt, and sometimes fade into obscurity. Yet they survive through inheritance. Latin, though no longer a spoken language in common life, still informs modern law, science, and theology. In a parallel sense, programming languages function as mediums through which human thought is immortalized. A program written in Fortran or Lisp does not disappear simply because trends shift toward newer languages. Instead, it remains as an artifact that future generations must either preserve, translate, or replace. The legacy of language in human culture mirrors the legacy of code in digital culture. Both serve as vessels of thought that outlive their authors. Inheritance in systems is not merely a technical issue but a profound human one. To inherit a body of code is to inherit the thought processes, design assumptions, and cultural biases of those who wrote it.

Code is not neutral. It embodies the context of its creation. A system developed in the 1970s reflects the computational limitations, architectural paradigms, and philosophical assumptions of its era. For example, the design of mainframe applications assumes centralized processing power, while modern distributed systems assume ubiquitous connectivity. Each generation of code reflects its historical moment, but through inheritance, it also imposes those assumptions on the future. To maintain a legacy system is to wrestle with the ghosts of past choices.

The weight of this inheritance is often underestimated. Engineers entering a company rarely encounter clean slates. Instead, they are tasked with understanding millions of lines of code written long before their arrival. Each line carries intent, but not always clarity. Each function embodies a solution, but not always one aligned with present needs. To inherit code is to engage in archaeology. One digs through layers of logic, documentation, and sometimes silence. Comments left by previous developers serve as inscriptions, clues to intent. Missing documentation becomes voids where meaning must be reconstructed. This process reveals that code, like ancient manuscripts, is as much about deciphering as it is about executing. Yet the inheritance of systems is not purely burdensome. It also represents continuity. When a piece of code is preserved, it becomes a link in a chain of intellectual history. The developer who maintains an old program is not merely patching bugs but participating in a lineage of thought. Just as a mathematician builds upon the theorems of predecessors, software engineers build upon architectures that predate them. The continuity of systems creates stability in a world of rapid change. Financial institutions cannot afford to rebuild every decade. Healthcare cannot pause to modernize from scratch. In these contexts, the inheritance of code ensures reliability. The weight of inheritance, while heavy, provides the backbone of continuity. The language of systems, therefore, becomes a language of inheritance. Developers writing today are not writing for themselves alone. They are writing for the unseen inheritors who will one day read, interpret, and extend their work. This perspective should transform the way we think about systems design. Code is not just functional; it is communicative. It must speak clearly not only to machines but to the humans who inherit it. A function name, a variable, a comment, or a structural choice carries meaning that transcends execution. To write code with permanence is to write with clarity, empathy, and foresight. The weight of inheritance also raises questions about responsibility. When a system fails decades after it was written, who bears responsibility? Is it the original author, whose decisions set the framework? Is it the inheritor, who failed to adapt it properly? Or is it the organization that neglected to invest in modernization? The answer is complex, but what is clear is that inheritance magnifies the stakes of authorship. To write code is to shape not only the present but the future. The permanence of systems means that every decision echoes forward in time.

This permanence becomes especially striking when systems outlive their creators in the literal sense. Many systems in use today were written by individuals who have passed away. Yet their code continues to run, shaping economies and institutions. This phenomenon blurs the line between life and legacy. In literature, an author may be remembered through their books. In architecture, a designer may be remembered through their buildings. In software, a developer is remembered through systems that continue to function long after their passing. This digital afterlife of thought makes code a unique medium of legacy. To understand the weight of inheritance is also to understand the fragility of permanence. A system may persist, but its survival is not guaranteed. Without careful stewardship, code can become incomprehensible, insecure, or unusable. The permanence of systems depends on the capacity of humans to interpret and maintain them. Just as ancient texts require translation and preservation, legacy systems require active care. Without it, permanence collapses into obsolescence. The inheritance of systems is therefore not passive but active. It requires engagement, adaptation, and renewal. At its core, the language of systems and the weight of inheritance remind us that coding is never an isolated act. It is part of a continuum, a dialogue across time. The permanence of systems transforms coding into authorship and inheritance into interpretation. Every line of code written today carries the potential to outlive its author, shaping the digital and social landscapes of tomorrow. The responsibility of this reality should not burden developers into paralysis but inspire them toward clarity, empathy, and vision. Systems endure not because of their novelty but because of their ability to be understood, maintained, and extended by those who inherit them. This truth redefines the role of the developer. To write code is not only to solve problems but to communicate across generations. It is to craft a language that carries meaning forward, a structure that will hold weight beyond its original moment. The inheritance of systems is both challenge and opportunity. It is heavy with the past yet full of potential for the future. In recognizing this, we begin to see coding not as transient execution but as enduring authorship, a form of writing that secures permanence through the weight of inheritance.

The Philosophy of Longevity in Code

The philosophy of longevity in code begins with a recognition that software is not merely a functional instrument but a crafted vessel of thought that is meant to endure far beyond its initial context. When a developer writes code, they are engaging in an act of intellectual projection, one that anticipates a future where others may rely on their logic, their structure, and their choices in design. The pursuit of longevity in code asks the creator to step outside the urgency of the present and consider how their work will resonate years or even decades after its conception. This is not about predicting technological futures with precision but about creating with a discipline that favors clarity, adaptability, and resilience over temporary expedience. The philosophy here is not grounded in perfection but in a responsible humility that recognizes the enduring consequences of design decisions. At the core of this philosophy lies the belief that code is a living text. Like a manuscript, it communicates not only what is necessary for its immediate execution but also what is required for its comprehension by future interpreters. The syntax and structure carry meaning for compilers and processors, but the comments, the modularity, and the organization carry meaning for human beings who must sustain it. Longevity in code therefore exists at the intersection of two audiences, one machine and one human, both of which must be satisfied if the code is to survive transitions in time, context, and utility. A philosophy of longevity prioritizes this dual responsibility, asking the developer to see themselves not as a temporary problem solver but as an author contributing to a tradition. To write for permanence demands more than technical competence. It requires an ethos of stewardship. Systems that endure are rarely those that are flashy in their moment of creation. They are often humble in their appearance, unadorned by the complexities of fashionable trends but marked by a disciplined simplicity that allows them to be adapted without breaking. This simplicity does not mean a lack of depth but rather a conscious restraint, a recognition that every additional layer of complexity becomes a potential burden for those who must inherit it. Longevity in code is inextricably tied to this balance between present ambition and future responsibility. It is a choice to prioritize stability over novelty, structure over improvisation, and communication over obscurity. Historical patterns reinforce this truth. The languages and systems that have endured across decades are rarely those that were designed for the sake of spectacle. They were designed with principles that centered clarity, portability, and universality. Consider the persistence of languages like C or Python. Their resilience does not stem from their ability to do everything at once but from their ability to do core things well while remaining legible to a wide community. They were not frozen in time but were constructed with foundations that could evolve without collapsing. The philosophy of longevity in code asks developers to view their own creations with the same discipline, ensuring that what they build is not brittle but adaptable, not locked into a narrow present but open to broader futures.

There is a moral dimension embedded in this philosophy. When one creates systems that others must rely upon, there is an ethical duty to ensure that the system is not fragile. Fragility may serve immediate deadlines, but it ultimately imposes costs upon future maintainers, who inherit both the utility and the flaws of the system. Longevity in code acknowledges that while the original author may not be present, their influence remains embedded in every function, every decision, every hidden assumption. To write for endurance is to recognize this ethical footprint and to take seriously the weight of technological inheritance. Each line of code becomes a signature not just of skill but of responsibility.

This sense of responsibility also transforms how one perceives complexity. Complexity is not inherently destructive, but unmanaged complexity is corrosive. Systems that aspire to longevity must account for complexity in measured ways. They must create layers of abstraction that are transparent rather than obscure, pathways of modification that are predictable rather than chaotic, and patterns of reuse that empower rather than constrain. Longevity demands that complexity be tamed, not eliminated, so that it remains a source of power rather than a liability. The philosophical stance here is not to shy away from intricate systems but to shape them with intentional design that honors both present and future needs. Another dimension of this philosophy is cultural. Longevity in code cannot exist in isolation from the communities that sustain it. Systems outlive their creators because they are taken up, interpreted, modified, and expanded by collectives of developers who see value in them. The philosophy of longevity acknowledges this communal dimension and seeks to foster environments where knowledge is shared, documentation is valued, and collaboration is prioritized. Code that is written with longevity in mind becomes a shared text, a living archive that grows richer with every contribution. In this sense, longevity is not simply a technical achievement but a cultural one, a product of collective stewardship rather than solitary genius. The implications of this philosophy reach beyond programming. To create enduring code is to participate in a broader human pursuit of legacy. Just as architects design structures to outlast generations and authors compose texts to carry ideas beyond their lifetimes, developers create systems that embody their intellectual imprint in the digital realm. Longevity in code is a mirror of longevity in thought, an acknowledgment that human creativity finds its highest form not in fleeting novelty but in sustainable contribution. In this view, code is not only an instrument of immediate utility but also a medium of memory, a channel through which future generations may engage with the logic and imagination of those who came before them.

The pursuit of this philosophy requires courage, because it often runs against the grain of rapid development cycles and short-term demands. In many environments, the pressure to deliver quickly outweighs the discipline to deliver well. To insist upon longevity is to resist this pressure, to hold fast to the conviction that what is built should not merely function today but endure tomorrow. It is a discipline that may seem costly in the present but that yields immense value in the long arc of time. Systems that are rushed into existence may shine briefly but will collapse under the weight of their own neglect. Systems that are built with longevity in mind will not only survive but will provide a foundation upon which future innovation can thrive. Ultimately, the philosophy of longevity in code is an invitation to imagine the future not as an abstract horizon but as a concrete reality that will be shaped by the decisions of today. It challenges developers to write with vision, to architect with humility, and to code with a sense of responsibility that transcends their immediate context. In embracing this philosophy, code ceases to be a disposable artifact and becomes instead a lasting legacy, a contribution to the ongoing narrative of human ingenuity.

Beyond the Author: Systems as Living Memory

When code transcends the immediate purpose of solving a task, when it stretches beyond the narrow horizon of the author who typed the first line, it becomes something far greater than mere instructions to a machine. It becomes a form of memory, a living artifact that captures thought, process, and vision. To understand software as living memory requires us to detach it from the mechanics of syntax and recognize it instead as a cultural and intellectual archive. It does not only execute; it remembers. Every choice that a developer makes, every design pattern, every library imported, and every structure created reflects the mental framework of the person who authored it. Yet once the code exists within the ecosystem of others, once it is pushed into repositories, integrated into frameworks, and depended upon by future projects, it ceases to belong solely to its originator. It becomes a shared resource and a collective inheritance. When looking at systems that endure, one observes that they begin to function as vessels of human continuity. Think of the foundational operating systems or the programming languages that continue to power modern infrastructures decades after their creation. They contain not only logic but also a philosophy. They are repositories of assumptions about how humans should interact with machines, about how data should be stored, transferred, and manipulated, about how complexity should be managed. In this way, code is not just written instruction but a record of a worldview. When future engineers interact with such systems, they are engaging with an embedded memory of earlier generations. They are conversing with the minds of those who laid the foundations even if those voices are long silent.

The idea of systems as living memory resonates with the deeper patterns of civilization. Just as manuscripts, oral traditions, and monuments carry forward the essence of human societies, so too do technological artifacts capture the spirit of their creators. Yet unlike static inscriptions or relics, software possesses dynamism. It executes, evolves, adapts, and integrates. This dynamism allows it to remain relevant and functional, ensuring that the memory embedded in its architecture is not frozen but active.

The system itself becomes alive not in the biological sense but in its capacity to act, respond, and continue serving roles unforeseen by its originators. This phenomenon of living memory raises profound questions about authorship and ownership. Who owns the memory of a system once it passes into collective use? The original creator may retain their name in documentation, but the system becomes a field of interaction where countless contributors modify and extend it. Each addition layers new memory upon the old, creating a palimpsest of thought. The code is no longer the isolated artifact of a single person. It becomes a cultural record composed through collaboration across time. The persistence of Unix, for example, shows how an architecture designed in the 1970s could continue to thrive, absorbing new technologies while maintaining its core philosophy. The living memory of Unix lies not only in its code but in its design principles which countless engineers have internalized and replicated. When systems become living memory, they also create continuity across discontinuity. The individuals who built them may retire, change careers, or pass away, yet the code remains to speak for them. Even as companies dissolve and technologies shift, the memory encoded in these systems does not vanish. It can be forked, ported, and adapted into new contexts. This continuity ensures that ideas which were once localized in particular times and places achieve universality.

The living memory encoded in software outlasts institutions, industries, and even paradigms of technology itself.

The persistence of systems as memory also demonstrates the ethical weight borne by creators. When you write code that will be inherited, you are not only solving a problem but encoding values and structures that others will depend on. Poor design choices, unethical assumptions, or negligence can poison the inheritance, leaving behind a memory that is harmful rather than empowering. Conversely, careful design, clarity of documentation, and an openness to extension ensure that the memory passed on is one of generosity and foresight. In this way, every line of code is an ethical act. It is a decision about the kind of memory you will leave behind and the kind of interaction you will invite others into long after you are gone. Another dimension of systems as living memory is their role in education. Beginners learn to program not only by studying abstract syntax but by reading existing systems. They inherit habits of thought, design strategies, and cultural attitudes toward coding through exposure to systems that have persisted. When they see how older systems were constructed, they are learning from the memory encoded in them. Thus, systems become pedagogical artifacts. They teach silently by embodying principles that would otherwise require decades of experience to articulate. In this way, the memory of the system becomes a teacher across generations. Furthermore, when systems achieve this state of memory, they invite reinterpretation. Each generation of programmers re-encounters the system with fresh eyes, bringing new challenges and needs. They may find limitations in the code, but even those limitations carry memory. They reveal what was once possible, what was once considered important, and what constraints shaped the original design. To work within these systems is to converse with the past, to wrestle with it, to reinterpret it, and to push it forward into the future. This is why so many enduring systems carry with them a sense of heritage. Working with them feels like joining a lineage rather than beginning anew.

The endurance of memory in code also illustrates the paradox of permanence within impermanence. On the one hand, software is fragile, prone to obsolescence, and dependent on hardware that itself changes rapidly. On the other hand, the conceptual memory encoded in its architecture can persist indefinitely. For instance, while specific implementations may fade, the underlying philosophies continue to inspire new generations of systems. The relational database model conceived decades ago still underpins vast swathes of modern computing, even though the original implementations may no longer be in use. Thus, memory outlives medium, and ideas achieve a kind of permanence beyond their immediate technical form. There is also a social dimension to systems like living memory. Communities form around enduring codebases, sustaining them, defending them, and extending them. These communities act as stewards of memory.

They ensure that knowledge is not lost and that the memory remains accessible to newcomers. This stewardship transforms the code into more than technical artifact. It becomes a cultural home, a gathering point where shared identity is constructed. This is evident in the open-source world where communities preserve and extend code for decades, not because it is always efficient or modern, but because it is memory worth keeping alive.

When reflecting on systems as living memory, one must also recognize the burden they place on the future. Inheriting code is never neutral. It requires understanding, adaptation, and often reconciliation with outdated assumptions. This is why legacy systems, while invaluable, can also be challenging. They carry forward memory, but memory that may not always align with current needs. Yet even in their difficulties, they testify to the persistence of human thought. They remind us that we are never building in a vacuum but always inheriting from those who came before. Ultimately, to view systems as living memory is to reframe our understanding of technology itself. Technology is not merely tools. It is memory in motion. It carries the presence of its creators into futures they could not imagine. It allows dialogue across generations, enabling us to learn from voices long absent and to leave traces of our own thinking for those yet to come. To write code is therefore not only an act of engineering but of remembrance and anticipation. It is to contribute to the ongoing archive of human ingenuity. It is to inscribe thought into a medium that, while fragile in one sense, can endure in another far longer than flesh or stone.

The legacy of systems as living memory is profound. It reminds us that we are participants in an unbroken chain of thought stretching from the first punched cards to the most sophisticated distributed systems of today. Every keystroke is a contribution to this chain, every repository a node in the great network of memory. As long as systems persist, so too does the presence of their creators, echoing silently through the functions, classes, and architectures they left behind. To write code is to plant memory. To sustain systems is to tend memory. And to inherit code is to converse with the living past.

Chapter Three

Systems as Foundations of Collective Knowledge

The civilizations of the world are remembered not merely by the monuments they built but by the systems of thought they left behind. In the same way that languages, scripts, and mathematical frameworks become the scaffolding of cultural endurance, code emerges as the twenty first century's universal structure for organizing collective memory. When we look back at the evolution of human progress, what truly survived was not the individual rulers or inventors but the systems that translated their innovations into a usable form for those who came after them. Writing systems, legal codes, number systems, and scientific methods each became the arteries through which civilization transported its inheritance across centuries. In our era code occupies this same stature. It is not simply an instruction to machines. It is an architecture for thought, a vessel for collective continuity, and a foundation upon which the modern digital civilization rests. To understand this dimension of code we must first confront the nature of collective knowledge itself. Knowledge is rarely the work of a single mind operating in isolation. It is instead the layered sediment of countless contributions, arguments, and refinements over time. When Euclid systematized geometry, he was not creating something from nothing. He was synthesizing the work of Egyptian surveyors, Babylonian astronomers, and earlier Greek mathematicians into a coherent structure. That structure survived not because Euclid was extraordinary but because the system was transmissible. In much the same way code gains its permanence when it becomes a shared system that others can adopt, extend, and adapt. The weight of inheritance is carried not by the brilliance of a single developer but by the ability of a system to encode logic in such a way that future generations can inhabit it. Thus, the act of writing code is also the act of building a civilization of logic.

Civilizations rise and fall, but the structures that endure are those that achieve universality. Consider the decimal number system. Its endurance is not tied to its inventors but to its ability to integrate into any culture that values mathematics. The same can be said of programming languages and frameworks. When they provide not just a tool for the moment but a structure capable of supporting countless contexts, they outlive their creators. Think of how C became the invisible foundation of operating systems, databases, and languages that dominate the present. Its syntax, though devised decades ago, still governs the way entire generations of programmers think. This is what it means for code to function as civilization. It has become an intellectual infrastructure so deeply embedded that its absence is unimaginable. To build systems that embody collective knowledge requires humility. A developer must recognize that the most important measure of code is not how clever it is in the moment but how usable it is in the future. Systems that prioritize clarity, structure, and adaptability offer the same gift that great cultural artifacts offer: the possibility of inheritance. In this way software architecture resembles the architecture of cities. A city built only for immediate use collapses when its circumstances change. A city designed with foresight, with avenues for expansion, with spaces for integration of the new, becomes a living organism that grows with its inhabitants. Code written with foresight achieves the same permanence. It allows future generations to inhabit it, transform it, and expand it without tearing it apart entirely. This recognition transforms the role of the developer into that of a cultural custodian. Each line of code carries not only functional logic but the potential to either restrict or empower those who will come after. Poorly designed systems become prisons of maintenance, where future developers are trapped in the inefficiencies of the past. Well-designed systems become cathedrals of logic, where every extension feels like a natural continuation of what came before. The difference is not in the cleverness of the solution but in the recognition that code is more than a technical artifact. It is a cultural foundation. It is a language in which civilization negotiates its continuity. To treat code as civilization also requires confronting the fragility of digital systems. Unlike stone monuments or papyrus manuscripts, digital systems are ephemeral without deliberate preservation. A program written in the 1960s may still exist, but it requires interpreters, emulators, and careful stewardship to remain alive. Civilization demands maintenance. This is why documentation, open standards, and transparent architectures are essential. They ensure that the inheritance of code does not vanish when its original environment disappears. Just as civilizations build libraries, archives, and traditions of scholarship to safeguard their knowledge, developers must build documentation, repositories, and communities of practice to safeguard their systems. The survival of code is never guaranteed. It must be cultivated with the same seriousness as any cultural artifact. The metaphor of code as civilization also reveals why collaboration is essential. No civilization is built by a single hand. It requires communities of builders, scholars, and practitioners who together sustain the architecture of thought. Open source embodies this principle. It transforms individual contributions into a collective system where thousands of voices create structures that outlive their original contexts. The Linux kernel, for example, is not the work of one person but of a civilization of developers whose shared contributions have built an operating system that powers the modern internet, smartphones, and countless machines. This is not merely a technical triumph. It is a civilizational achievement. It demonstrates that code can be the organizing principle of a society of builders. We should also consider the ethical responsibilities of treating code as civilization. Civilizations are remembered not only for their technical achievements but also for the values they encoded in their systems. The Roman Empire left behind roads and laws but also hierarchies and exclusions. The systems of the digital civilization encode values. The choices developers make in designing platforms, algorithms, and infrastructures determine who benefits, who is excluded, and what futures are possible. To recognize code as civilization is to acknowledge that every decision in its architecture carries moral weight. Systems that prioritize openness, inclusivity, and adaptability enable a more just inheritance. Systems that prioritize secrecy, exploitation, or surveillance risk creating civilizations that collapse under the weight of their contradictions.

At its deepest level, treating code as civilization means understanding that we are always writing for the future. Every line is a message to those who will come after, just as every inscription, manuscript, and archive of past civilizations was a message to us. Some messages are easily understood. Others require immense effort to decode. The responsibility of the modern developer is to ensure that the messages encoded in code are not only functional but also comprehensible. Future civilizations of programmers will inherit the artifacts we leave behind. The question is whether we will leave them cathedrals of clarity or ruins of obscurity. This heading is a call to think beyond code as tool and to begin seeing it as the infrastructure of human continuity. Just as civilizations-built cities, laws, and languages that became the skeleton of their cultural existence, we today build code as the skeleton of the digital civilization. To dismiss its importance as mere technicality is to misunderstand the very foundation upon which the future will stand. Code is civilization not because it commands machines but because it organizes the life of billions of humans who depend on those machines. The inheritance of this civilization is being written line by line in repositories across the world. Its permanence depends on whether we recognize the magnitude of what we are building.

Systems as Invisible Cities

Code has often been compared to language, to mathematics, and to art, yet another fitting metaphor is that of cities that rise, flourish, and endure without most people ever seeing their foundations. When an architect draws lines on paper and the builders follow, a city rises in stone and concrete. In the realm of software, when a programmer writes instructions that machines follow, a digital city comes into existence. These cities are not visible to the eye, yet they structure the flow of commerce, the rhythm of communication, and the architecture of society itself. Systems behave like civilizations that exist within the shadows of daily life. Every time a person swipes a card at a store, checks a message, sends money across borders, or consults a medical record, they step into one of these invisible cities without realizing it. They walk its streets, depend on its electricity, and trust its water supply, even though these are not pipes and wires but protocols, databases, and networks. The developers who design these systems become the unseen urban planners of a digital civilization, embedding rules that millions will unconsciously follow. Unlike physical cities that reveal themselves in skyline and structure, these hidden civilizations operate behind screens, influencing economies and relationships without their citizens knowing the source of their order. The metaphor of the city is powerful because it conveys not only scale but permanence. A well-designed city can survive the deaths of its founders, just as a well-crafted system can live beyond the departure of its original coders. The Roman aqueducts still run through modern Europe, carrying water across miles with a precision that astonishes engineers. In similar fashion, code written decades ago continues to support global banks, airlines, and governments. The civilization it supports is invisible, but its durability is evident in the daily reliance placed upon it. The question that arises, then, is what principles make these digital cities endure while others collapse.

At the heart of systems as invisible cities is the balance between structure and flexibility. Too rigid a design and the city cannot grow with its citizens. Too loose a framework and the city becomes chaotic, unable to provide security or reliability. Programmers who think in terms of legacy must see themselves as urban planners of permanence. Their choices of architecture, language, and framework are not temporary but foundational, setting the paths along which future generations will walk. If they build poorly, collapse will come. If they build wisely, future innovators will inherit streets they can expand, bridges they can reinforce, and laws they can interpret in new contexts. The unseen civilization of code also raises questions of governance. Every civilization requires rules, written or unwritten, that regulate behavior. In digital cities, these rules are the protocols and standards that define communication between systems. When an application speaks to a server, when two services exchange data, when millions of devices synchronize, they are obeying the laws written by unseen legislators. These laws may appear technical, expressed in syntax and structure, yet they are as binding as the legal codes that govern physical societies. Breaking them leads to failure, incompatibility, or chaos. Maintaining them ensures order, growth, and trust. Yet unlike physical civilizations, digital ones rarely announce their rulers. The developers who first designed TCP or HTTP did not intend to be monarchs of global communication, but their work established the roads and bridges of the internet, and their influence endures long after their names fade. This invisibility both empowers and burdens those who write systems. Empowerment comes because their influence is vast and often unquestioned. Burden arises because their mistakes, once entrenched, become the inherited problems of generations. Just as urban planners may regret highways that divided communities or zoning laws that stifled growth, programmers may regret decisions that locked future systems into inefficiency or insecurity. The invisible city of code also introduces the idea of cultural memory. Every civilization develops traditions, rituals, and assumptions that its citizens absorb without question. In code, this memory is expressed in idioms, naming conventions, and architectural norms that persist even after their practical purpose fades. A modern system may contain lines of code that no one fully understands, yet they remain because they are part of the inherited culture of the system. Deleting them feels risky, preserving them feels safe, and thus the culture survives, even if its original meaning has been lost.

The permanence of these invisible civilizations demands a shift in mindset. Coders must realize they are not simply solving problems of the present moment but are establishing patterns that will guide the unseen lives of future generations. When a city is built, its streets dictate traffic for centuries. When code is written, its structures dictate workflows for decades. The invisible civilization is not simply an analogy but a reality, one in which the decisions of a few become the daily lived experience of millions who never knew those decisions were made. Thus, to think of systems as invisible cities is to acknowledge both the power and the responsibility of creating civilizations no one can see but everyone must inhabit. The permanence of these digital architectures demands humility, foresight, and care, for their influence outlives their creators and defines the future in ways no one can predict.

The Architecture of Permanence

When a coder begins to write, it may appear like a fleeting act, a moment of creativity producing lines on a screen. Yet if one looks deeply, the architecture they are shaping belongs to permanence rather than transience. The true measure of a system is not whether it works today but whether it can continue to support the lives of those who depend on it tomorrow. Code becomes a silent infrastructure, an unseen architecture upon which millions may lean without knowing. It ceases to be just logic or syntax and transforms into a scaffolding of permanence. The notion of permanence in digital architecture is complex because it does not imply immovability. In fact, permanence in software often depends on the ability to adapt without collapsing. Cities that endure for centuries do not do so by freezing in time but by evolving their use of space, their integration of culture, and their interpretation of tradition. Similarly, systems that survive decades are not those that remain untouched but those that allow themselves to be reinterpreted without losing their foundation. This delicate balance between rigidity and adaptability is the hallmark of architecture designed for permanence. Every architecture begins with decisions that appear small at the time but grow monumentally in consequence. The choice of programming language, the selection of frameworks, the organization of data, the method of handling failure become bricks and stones, some visible, others buried deep in the foundation. Just as a city may outgrow its walls or roads yet still depend on them for orientation, a system may evolve beyond its initial scope yet still remain bound by its earliest architectural choices. In the discipline of permanence, the smallest decisions echo the loudest. Consider the persistence of ancient aqueducts or the survival of medieval roads beneath modern highways. They were built not just with durability but with foresight, designed to outlast their builders. In the same way, systems that embody permanence are written with an awareness that the coder will one day vanish, but the code may continue to live. This awareness demands not only technical skill but humility, for permanence is not about the brilliance of the individual but about the capacity of the system to endure long after that individual is forgotten.

Architecture of permanence rests heavily on principles of simplicity and clarity. Complexity may impress in the short term but erodes in the long. A complex system is like a palace of mirrors: dazzling yet fragile. A simple, well-structured system is like a stone temple: unadorned but lasting. The coder who pursues permanence resists the temptation to dazzle and instead commits to clarity, for clarity invites understanding and understanding invites survival. Systems that are too complex become prisons of their own brilliance, accessible only to their creators and collapsing when those creators depart. Systems that are simple, however, become accessible to all who inherit them, adapting themselves across generations. Simplicity is not weakness but a foundation of resilience.

Another element of permanence is documentation, the equivalent of records and archives in a civilization. A city with no history cannot learn from its past, and a system with no documentation cannot survive the loss of its creators. Documentation is not glamorous, yet it is vital to permanence. It is the cultural memory of the architecture, the bridge that carries the system from one generation of coders to the next. Without it, the architecture becomes a ruin, functional perhaps but mysterious, forcing its inheritors to rebuild understanding rather than expand it. Thus, permanence demands not only building but storytelling. The builders must leave records of their intent, their methods, and their vision, so that those who follow can sustain rather than dismantle the work. Permanence also requires a philosophy of stewardship. The builders of cathedrals did not build for themselves but for generations they would never meet. Coders who build for permanence must adopt the same posture. They must see themselves as stewards of systems whose true users may not even be born yet. This mindset transforms the act of coding from one of solving immediate needs to one of crafting legacies. The coder who embraces stewardship avoids shortcuts that serve the present at the expense of the future. They write not to impress peers today but to empower strangers tomorrow. Such humility distinguishes temporary construction from enduring architecture. Furthermore, permanence is tested not by stability in calm moments but by resilience in crisis. Cities prove their strength not on days of peace but on days of flood, fire, or war. Systems prove their permanence not when everything works but when everything fails. Error handling, redundancy, fault tolerance are not mere technical features but principles of survival. To write code that can endure failure is to acknowledge the inevitability of imperfection and to design not for the absence of error but for its inevitability. A permanent system does not deny failure; it absorbs it and continues.

The architecture of permanence is also political, for permanence implies influence, and influence implies responsibility. Just as the layout of a city influences the lives of its citizens, the architecture of a system influences the behavior of its users. The way data is stored, the way permissions are structured, the way interfaces are designed, these are not neutral choices but decisions that shape human behavior. Permanence in architecture therefore carries ethical weight. A system that endures while enabling harm becomes a monument to negligence rather than wisdom. True permanence demands not only technical excellence but moral foresight, ensuring that the system that survives contributes to the flourishing rather than the exploitation of those who depend on it. In addition, permanence invites the question of legacy. When builders raise monuments, when artists create works of stone or bronze, they hope that time will preserve their vision. Coders rarely imagine their work as monuments, yet permanence transforms their code into precisely that. Millions may walk daily through the invisible corridors they built, just as tourists wander through ancient ruins. The permanence of architecture is not measured by how long the coder remembers but by how long the world unknowingly depends upon it. Legacy is not an intentional pursuit but an inevitable consequence of permanence. Ultimately, the architecture of permanence is not about creating systems that never change but about creating systems that never collapse under change. It is about designing invisible cathedrals, unseen aqueducts, and hidden roads upon which future generations will live without ever seeing the builders. It is about accepting that permanence is both power and burden, for to build something that lasts is to surrender control of it to the unknown. Yet this surrender is precisely what transforms ordinary coding into extraordinary legacy.

Chapter Four

Systems as Narratives of Human Intention

When we consider the idea of code as a permanent structure, the first notion that arises is the reality that every system ever written carries the fingerprint of its author. This fingerprint is not just a reflection of syntax or style but an encapsulation of human intention projected into a framework that others can engage with long after the originator has left the scene. Code becomes more than a utilitarian expression of logic. It transforms into narrative, into a story told line by line that carries within it the burdens, assumptions, visions, and philosophies of the one who created it. When seen in this way, a program is no longer simply an instrument to execute functionality. It is instead an archive of choices, values, and perspectives encoded into the architecture of digital life. The act of writing code has often been described as a conversation between human and machine, where the human attempts to communicate ideas with a precision that can be executed by silicon without error or ambiguity. Yet if we stretch this view further, code can also be seen as a conversation between human and time. The author speaks not only to the machine in front of them but to the generations of developers, users, and systems that will eventually inherit this work. Every class, every function, every structure becomes an intentional or unintentional message delivered forward into an era the original author may never see. This is why code must be understood as a narrative. It is not merely a static construct but a dynamic account of how one person or one collective thought the world should be organized at a given moment in history.

Within this narrative quality lies the weight of inheritance. Future developers inherit not only the logical framework of a system but also the philosophical assumptions embedded within it. For instance, when we look at the architecture of early programming languages, we find that their creators encoded certain beliefs about how humans should interact with machines. Assembly language assumed a closeness to the machine, forcing the programmer to think in binary and hexadecimal, teaching them to respect the intricacies of hardware. High level languages like C and later Python carried an entirely different assumption, that abstraction and accessibility should empower human creativity rather than bind it to mechanical detail. These decisions reveal the stories of their creators, and those stories then ripple across decades of usage and adaptation. The inheritance is not passive. It is an active force shaping how future systems evolve. When a developer maintains or extends code, they often find themselves wrestling with decisions made years earlier. Why did the author structure the data in this way? Why was this method chosen instead of another? What tradeoffs did they accept? In answering these questions, one does not merely decode logic but deciphers intention. Maintenance then becomes not unlike archaeology, where the coder unearths layers of reasoning and reconstructs the worldview of a previous thinker. In this sense, code is not just technical legacy but cultural heritage, handed down across time through the medium of logic and execution. There is also a deeper philosophical tension within this narrative quality of systems. On one hand, the author strives for clarity, universality, and timelessness, hoping that their code will remain readable and functional for years to come. On the other hand, every author is a creature of their time, influenced by the technologies, paradigms, and limitations of their era. Thus, every codebase is simultaneously timeless, and time bound. It carries aspirations to endure but also betrays the fingerprints of its historical moment. The punch card systems of the mid twentieth century told the story of scarcity, when memory and processing power were precious commodities. The sprawling web frameworks of today tell the story of abundance, when connectivity and cloud power allow experimentation without the same constraints. Systems, therefore, can be read like historical documents. They speak not only of technical goals but of human context. To study the architecture of an old operating system is to glimpse how its creators viewed hierarchy, control, and modularity. To examine the structure of a large open-source project is to glimpse how its contributors' imagined collaboration, ownership, and governance. Just as literature reveals the concerns and imaginations of its era, code reveals the implicit philosophies of those who shaped it. Yet unlike literature, code is rarely treated with reverence. Too often, it is discarded, rewritten, or patched without recognition of its narrative weight. But if code is truly a narrative of human intention, then discarding it lightly is akin to erasing a story that once carried meaning. This is why the preservation of legacy systems, even those no longer actively used, matters for more than nostalgic reasons. They serve as living museums of thought, reminding us of the paths once taken, the mistakes once made, and the victories once earned. Without these reminders, we risk repeating the same cycles of error, reinventing solutions already found, or forgetting the lessons written in the logic of the past.

At the same time, narratives carried in systems are not static artifacts. They evolve as they are interpreted, rewritten, and expanded by those who inherit them. A piece of code written in the 1980s may be extended by a developer in the 2000s who brings their own worldview into the system. Layers of intention accumulate, turning the system into a palimpsest of human thought. Each layer does not fully erase the previous one but adds new meaning, new functionality, and new interpretations. This process mirrors how cultures evolve through the reinterpretation of texts, traditions, and practices. Systems too are cultural texts, continuously rewritten but always carrying echoes of their origins. To view systems as narratives of human intention also shifts how we approach design. If every program is a story, then writing code becomes not only an act of engineering but also an act of authorship. The programmer is not merely building functionality. They are crafting a story that will be read by future programmers, interpreted by future machines, and lived by future users. This recognition imposes responsibility. It demands that programmers consider not only what works today but what will remain coherent tomorrow. Just as a writer edits their prose for clarity so that future readers will not misunderstand, a programmer must shape their structures for transparency so that future maintainers will not lose their way. Narratives also raise the question of voice. Whose intention is truly captured in a system? In large projects, thousands of contributors may touch the code, each leaving their imprint. The resulting narrative becomes a chorus rather than a solo performance, a collective story shaped by many voices. Yet even in such collectives, patterns of intention emerge. Leadership choices, community norms, and cultural biases shape the story told by the system. This is why studying open-source projects reveals not only technical insights but also sociological ones. The governance model, the documentation practices, and the inclusivity of contributions all influence the kind of story that system will carry into the future.

There is a poetic irony in all this. Many coders approach their work with a sense of impermanence, believing that their systems will soon be replaced, refactored, or rewritten. And yet history shows that code often outlives its authors in ways they could never predict. Systems written as temporary solutions persist for decades, while ambitious projects designed for longevity sometimes fade quickly. The difference lies not only in technical merit but in how well the story resonates with future generations. Like literature, some code is forgotten, while some becomes canonical. The inheritance of systems is therefore unpredictable, shaped by forces far beyond the original author's control. This uncertainty should not discourage but inspire. If the story of code can echo beyond its expected lifespan, then every act of authorship carries the possibility of legacy. Even a simple script may one day become foundational to a larger system. Even a modest contribution may shape the habits of future developers. Thus, the weight of inheritance rests not only on monumental works but also on the smallest fragments of intention. Every function is a sentence, every module, a chapter, every system, a book in the library of digital history. The narrative quality of systems also explains why communities form around code. People are drawn not only to the functionality of a system but to the story it tells. They find meaning in the elegance of its architecture, the philosophy of its design, or the culture of its contributors. These stories give identity to projects, allowing them to inspire loyalty and passion. In this sense, code becomes a social text, binding individuals into communities that transcend geography and time. The inheritance is not only technical but communal, as the story continues to live through those who adopt and extend it. Ultimately, to understand systems as narratives of human intention is to elevate the act of programming from mere engineering to cultural authorship. It is to see code as both utility and text, both logic and story, both machine instruction and human philosophy. When we write code, we are not only solving problems. We are writing stories that future generations will inherit, interpret, and extend. We are participating in an eternal dialogue between code and time, where every line written is a sentence in a book that will outlive us.

The Responsibility of Code as Cultural Heritage

When one thinks of heritage, images of monuments, libraries, and artifacts usually surface before anything as intangible as code. Yet if one looks deeper into the fabric of modern civilization, it becomes evident that code has already surpassed many traditional markers of cultural memory. Entire generations will not remember buildings or statues as vividly as they remember the platforms, tools, and digital environments that defined their daily existence. Code has woven itself into the continuity of human history, and with that presence comes an undeniable responsibility. Those who write code do not merely craft functionality, they craft culture, and in crafting culture, they inherit the duty of stewardship toward posterity. The act of treating code as cultural heritage demands a shift in both perception and practice. For centuries, the guardians of cultural heritage were archivists, historians, and curators, tasked with ensuring the longevity of physical objects. But in the digital era, software engineers, system architects, and open-source communities have inherited a parallel role. They safeguard not stone carvings or ancient manuscripts but digital expressions of human ingenuity. Code is written in languages designed for machines, but its echoes belong to humanity. The structures, paradigms, and frameworks that shape the digital sphere will be remembered not only for their technical brilliance but also for their social, ethical, and historical impact. If one accepts this premise, then the responsibility of writing code is no longer confined to efficiency, scalability, and speed. It stretches into the realm of ethics, sustainability, and inclusivity. For instance, the choice of whether to build software that prioritizes accessibility is not a mere engineering concern but a cultural decision. Software that excludes people with disabilities from digital participation denies them entry into the living culture of the digital age. Thus, accessibility in code is not just about compliance with regulations but about protecting cultural equity. A programmer who dismisses accessibility disregards the fact that code is not neutral. It is as culturally loaded as a novel, a film, or a constitution.

In examining the responsibility of code as heritage, one cannot ignore the concept of digital decay. Just as parchment deteriorates and monuments erode, digital systems risk obsolescence. The rapid pace of technological innovation creates an environment where even well-built software can become unreadable within decades. Languages fall out of favor, platforms become unsupported, and hardware architectures evolve beyond recognition. Unlike a stone tablet that can be deciphered thousands of years later, a piece of software written in a forgotten language risks permanent silence. This raises the question of preservation. How do we ensure that future generations can access the digital artifacts we build today? Preservation of code is not a passive endeavor. It requires intentional strategies such as open standards, comprehensive documentation, and long-term archival efforts. The work of organizations like the Internet Archive demonstrates the urgency of digital preservation. By archiving websites, programs, and digital objects, they act as cultural guardians of the digital frontier. Yet the responsibility cannot rest solely on institutions. Developers themselves must adopt the mindset that their work may someday be studied as heritage. This means leaving behind not only code that works but also code that speaks, code that tells its story through clarity, structure, and purpose. Just as an architect considers how future generations will view a building, so must the software engineer consider how the traces of their logic will shape the understanding of digital culture centuries from now.

This responsibility becomes even more profound when viewed through the lens of open source. Open-source code is one of the most significant cultural contributions of the modern world. It is not locked in vaults or museums but lives as a dynamic, evolving heritage accessible to anyone. The open-source ethos mirrors the tradition of libraries and academies, where knowledge was shared for the collective progress of humanity. Every contribution to an open-source project is a statement that knowledge belongs not to the few but to the many. However, with this openness comes a heightened responsibility. The decisions made within open-source communities reverberate widely, shaping not only immediate users but also the course of technological evolution. The sustainability of such projects is therefore not merely a question of technical upkeep but of cultural stewardship. Equally important is the recognition of marginalized voices in the heritage of code. Too often, the history of computing is told through the names of a few celebrated figures, while the contributions of women, minorities, and underrepresented communities are overlooked. Yet the cultural value of code cannot be separated from the inclusivity of its narrative. o truly preserve code as heritage, one must also preserve the stories of those who wrote it, the communities who shaped it, and the users whose lives it touched. Otherwise, we risk leaving behind an incomplete memory of the digital age, a memory that favors power and privilege over diversity and humanity. The ethical dimensions of this responsibility stretch even further when one considers the environmental cost of code. Every piece of software carries an ecological footprint, tied to the energy required to run, maintain, and scale it. Code that is bloated, inefficient, or designed without sustainability in mind contributes to the broader strain on the environment. If code is heritage, then part of its value must be measured by the ecological burden it imposes. Future generations will not view our digital creations solely through the lens of functionality but also through the lens of environmental consequence. In this sense, efficient programming becomes not only a technical goal but a cultural and ecological duty. The tension between innovation and preservation complicates this responsibility further. Innovators naturally push boundaries, embracing new languages, paradigms, and platforms. Yet this constant forward momentum often discards what came before, creating a cycle of obsolescence that undermines cultural continuity. A balance must be struck between embracing the new and safeguarding the old. This is no different from how societies preserve ancient manuscripts while still producing new literature. The digital age must learn to cultivate both preservation and innovation simultaneously. This is why projects like emulators and digital archaeology are so vital. They allow modern users to interact with old systems while still benefiting from new advances. By bridging generations of technology, they create a continuum of heritage that resists the erasure of the past. It is also important to recognize that the responsibility of treating code as heritage extends to governance and policy. Governments and institutions must create frameworks that encourage digital preservation, fund cultural projects, and recognize software as part of the human record. Just as libraries receive public support because of their role in safeguarding culture, so too must digitally archives and preservation initiatives. Without systemic support, even the most well-intentioned developers and communities cannot guarantee the survival of their work across centuries. This is not a matter of convenience but of necessity. For future generations, the ability to study our digital heritage will be as crucial as the ability to study ancient texts and monuments has been for us. Finally, one must consider the profound human element at the core of this responsibility. Code is not written in a vacuum. It is the product of human minds, shaped by the contexts, struggles, and aspirations of its authors. To preserve code is to preserve human creativity, ingenuity, and identity. By treating code as cultural heritage, one acknowledges that humanity itself is reflected in every algorithm, every structure, every system. And in doing so, one affirms that writing code is not merely a technical act but a deeply human one, a continuation of the storytelling impulse that has defined civilization since its earliest days. If future generations are to inherit a digital world that reflects the full richness of human thought, the coders of today must embrace this responsibility. They must write with clarity, preserve with intent, and act with humility, knowing that their work will outlive them. For in the end, code is not only a set of instructions for machines. It is a cultural text, a monument of logic, and a legacy that must be handed down with care.

Designing for Tomorrow While Living in Today

The creation of code is never fully situated in the present moment. Even though it may arise from immediate needs and is influenced by the constraints of current technologies, its destiny often stretches far beyond the lifetime of its author. Each line carries within it the weight of foresight, whether conscious or unconscious, because software is never only about what it accomplishes today but also about the possibilities it enables or limits tomorrow. To design systems that live beyond the present moment is to recognize the tension between urgency and permanence, between the immediate function and the enduring form. This duality defines the essence of sustainable coding. When a developer writes for a deadline, there is the temptation to optimize for short term execution, focusing on quick delivery and temporary results. Yet the systems that achieve immortality are those that embrace a different logic, one that acknowledges that code will be read more times than it is written, that software will evolve in contexts the original author cannot anticipate, and that the users of tomorrow may demand functions that today's designers could not imagine. Designing for tomorrow while living in today requires the acceptance of uncertainty as the natural state of technology. Every enduring system begins as a compromise between vision and necessity. The present imposes limitations: hardware has finite memory, networks operate with constraints, business needs insist on deadlines. Within these boundaries, the architect of code must still find ways to construct something elastic, something that can stretch into futures not yet revealed. It is this elasticity that transforms temporary solutions into permanent legacies. The most significant technologies of history did not emerge because their authors knew exactly how they would be used in the future, but because they created frameworks open enough to accommodate new interpretations.

Consider the structure of the Internet. When its foundations were laid in the middle of the twentieth century, its architects were addressing the problem of resilient communication networks. They did not envision social media platforms, global e commerce, or video streaming, yet the principles of packet switching, distributed communication, and standardized protocols allowed for a universe of future possibilities. The Internet became a stage upon which countless narratives could unfold. This is the core of designing for tomorrow: crafting not only what solves the problem today but also what opens paths to future use. However, to design for tomorrow does not mean neglecting the present. There is a delicate balance between foresight and pragmatism. A system too focused on hypothetical futures may never deliver meaningful value in the now, while a system bound to immediate concerns risks collapsing under the weight of irrelevance. The art lies in harmonizing both. It requires asking at every stage of design: What must this system accomplish now, and how can it be structured to evolve when tomorrow imposes new demands? Documentation becomes an essential companion in this pursuit. For future generations to maintain and adapt code, they must inherit not only the structure but also the thought process of its creators. A well-documented system becomes a bridge between eras. The author of today converses with the developer of tomorrow through carefully articulated reasoning. Without this bridge, code risks becoming an artifact too obscure to be preserved, an artifact that dies not because it lacks functionality but because it lacks accessibility. To design responsibly for the future also means considering ethical dimensions. Software carries immense influence on how societies function, how businesses operate, and how individuals live their lives. A system that persists beyond its original context can amplify both its virtues and its flaws. Biases coded unconsciously in the present may continue to shape outcomes long after the author is gone. This places a unique responsibility on designers: to create awareness, to test not only for functionality but also for fairness, and to recognize that their code is not just technical architecture but also cultural infrastructure. The legacy of software is most visible in the way systems outgrow their authors. A developer may no longer be alive, yet their logic persists in millions of devices, guiding interactions and decisions. In this sense, coding becomes a form of immortality. To live responsibly within this immortality requires humility. One must acknowledge that the future belongs not to the author but to the users, the maintainers, and the generations who will extend or restrict what has been given. Designing for tomorrow while living in today is therefore an act of stewardship. It is the recognition that systems are borrowed from the future even as they are created in the present. Scalability is a practical manifestation of this stewardship. A system built for today alone may work for a small group of users but collapse under the weight of growth. A system built with foresight anticipates expansion, both in terms of technical load and functional scope. This does not mean overengineering solutions to cover every imaginable case but rather building with modularity, with clarity, and with pathways for extension. Each component should be constructed as if it will one day be understood, reused, or rebuilt by someone who has never met the original author.

The tension between permanence and change is most visible in legacy code. Developers often speak of legacy systems with frustration, as burdens to be replaced. Yet this frustration often arises not from the fact that the system is old but from the fact that it was not designed to embrace change. True legacy is not defined by age but by adaptability. Systems that live gracefully across decades are those whose foundations allow for new layers, new integrations, and new languages without breaking under the pressure of progress. When designing for tomorrow, one must also consider the inevitability of obsolescence. No system can last forever in its original form. Hardware will evolve, new programming languages will emerge, user needs will transform. To design for permanence is not to resist this evolution but to anticipate it. A system that can be refactored, migrated, or reinterpreted is one that achieves endurance not by resisting change but by embracing it. This is why open standards, interoperable formats, and transparent structures are crucial. They are the seeds of continuity. In this sense, designing for tomorrow is not only a technical act but also a cultural one. It reflects the values of patience, humility, and generosity. It requires the developer to ask not only what the system can do but what it allows others to do. The systems that achieve timelessness are those that empower communities to carry them forward. They do not demand that the future bend to their rigidity; instead, they bend to the future.

To live today while designing for tomorrow means constantly negotiating with impermanence. It means coding as if the present matters and yet leaving doors open for futures that cannot be seen. It is to create with the awareness that what is temporary for the author may be permanent for society. This awareness transforms software from a product into a legacy. The most profound legacy of code lies not in its technical brilliance but in its ability to remain relevant across generations. A language, a framework, or a platform achieves permanence when it becomes a vessel through which human intentions continue to flow. It is not only a set of instructions but also a story, a memory, and an invitation to collaboration. This is what it means to design for tomorrow while living in today: to accept that every keystroke has the potential to echo across time, shaping futures that will never know the name of the one who typed it.

Chapter Five

Abstraction as the Bridge Between Ephemeral Code and Enduring Ideas

Abstraction has always been the silent force that allows human beings to transcend the immediate and the transient in order to reach for what lasts. In the realm of software this principle becomes even more profound because abstraction is what elevates raw instructions written for machines into frameworks of thought that can outlive their initial purpose. When a programmer decides to hide complexity behind a concept, when a structure is created to represent an idea rather than an operation, something extraordinary takes place. The code ceases to be only a set of technical directives and becomes instead a record of human reasoning, a crystallization of intent that can be understood by others long after the original author has departed.

The history of computing is marked by these moments of abstraction. Early programmers who dealt directly with machine instructions were burdened with fragility because every line was tied to specific hardware. There was little room for portability, and almost no room for interpretation beyond the immediate task. Yet with the birth of higher-level languages a new way of thinking emerged. Suddenly what was once a fleeting set of numbers meant only for a machine could be recast into statements that resembled human thought. A loop was no longer a series of jumps in binary but a representation of repetition that anyone could read and recognize. In this transformation code became more than execution. It became narrative. Abstraction therefore operates as a bridge, but not a fragile one. It is a bridge that allows ephemeral code to be carried forward into ideas that can survive across decades of technological change. Consider the simple abstraction of a function. To the computer it is ultimately just an address in memory and a sequence of instructions. But to a human reader it is a unit of thought, a named idea that encapsulates a behavior. When properly written, a function reveals what the programmer wanted to express in a way that far outlasts the hardware on which it runs. A sorting function written in the early days of computing could still be read and understood today, not because the original syntax remains fashionable, but because the abstraction behind it continues to hold power. Sorting is an eternal need, and the function becomes the artifact through which that need was addressed. The same is true for more complex abstractions. Data structures are not merely containers for bits of information. They are philosophies about how information should be arranged in relation to the world. A tree structure reflects the branching of decisions, of genealogies, of hierarchies that humanity has used for millennia. A graph reflects the intricate webs of relationships that connect entities in the real world. When these structures are encoded in software they become testaments of thought, embodiments of intellectual traditions. And because they exist as abstractions, they remain relevant even when the technologies of storage or computation change. The core idea survives because abstraction protects it from decay.

Yet abstraction does more than protect. It elevates. Through abstraction the act of programming shifts from mechanical labor into conceptual authorship. The programmer becomes less of an operator and more of an architect. The instructions given to the machine are important, but what truly endures is the architecture of thought built upon layers of abstraction. When we encounter legacy systems that still function after decades, we are not witnessing the survival of syntax. We are witnessing the endurance of abstractions that were carefully chosen and elegantly expressed. This is why abstraction is the invisible architecture of continuity. The ephemeral nature of raw code is undeniable. Machines change. Compilers evolve. Languages fall in and out of favor. But abstractions remain interpretable. They provide a timeless vocabulary that can be reimplemented, reimagined, and reborn across generations of technology. The structure of a loop, the encapsulation of behavior in functions, the organization of data into patterns, these are not confined to any particular machine. They are expressions of logic that transcend hardware and even transcend the lifetime of their authors. The act of abstraction also establishes a contract with the future. When a programmer designs a module with clarity, hiding unnecessary details and exposing only what is essential, they are speaking across time to future maintainers. They are saying here is the essence of what matters, everything else can change but this idea will remain. In doing so they create systems that can be understood and adapted, systems that can evolve while still preserving the original intent. This is the hallmark of legacy that matters, not the preservation of every line of code, but the transmission of the core idea through abstraction.

It is not accidental that some of the most enduring pieces of software are those that are built upon elegant abstractions. The Unix philosophy of small modular programs that do one thing well is an abstraction of simplicity and composability. It has survived decades not because the original shell scripts are still in use but because the abstraction they represented has been continually reinterpreted. The relational model of databases is another powerful example. Conceived as an abstraction of data and relationships, it has outlasted countless implementations. Even as storage technologies evolve the relational abstraction continues to guide how data is understood and manipulated.

One might argue that abstraction introduces distance, and that distance can lead to misunderstanding. After all, every abstraction hides details, and hidden details can eventually become pitfalls. This is true, yet it is precisely in this tension that legacy is shaped. Too little abstraction and the code is bound to perish with its machine. Too much abstraction and the code may lose contact with reality. The balance lies in crafting abstractions that are faithful to enduring truths while being flexible enough to survive change. It is this balance that transforms code into legacy.

Another dimension of abstraction is its social nature. Abstractions are not just technical constructs; they are agreements among people. A programming language is itself an abstraction, a collective agreement about how ideas should be expressed. Libraries and frameworks are abstractions that entire communities build upon. When these abstractions are adopted widely, they become cultural heritage within the field of software engineering. They create continuity not just across machines but across people. They allow knowledge to be shared, extended, and preserved. Think of the way object-oriented programming spread as an abstraction. It was not simply a new way of writing code. It was a new way of thinking about the world, about entities, behaviors, and relationships. The abstraction caught on because it resonated with how humans naturally perceive systems. It created a shared vocabulary that could be passed from one generation of programmers to another. That is why object-oriented principles are still taught and still applied, even as languages evolve. The abstraction became cultural memory.

Abstraction also reveals the human desire to be remembered not through physical monuments but through intellectual structures. When a mathematician formulates a theorem, the abstraction of that idea allows it to survive for centuries. Similarly, when a programmer writes code at the right level of abstraction, they contribute to an intellectual legacy that can endure beyond their lifetime. Their code may not survive in its literal form, but the abstractions they chose can influence generations of programmers who reinterpret them. This is the essence of code as legacy. The ephemeral lines may vanish, but the enduring abstractions remain as the true inheritance. When we study old codebases, we do not marvel at the syntax, we marvel at the thought patterns embedded within. We see how someone long ago grappled with complexity, how they chose to structure their ideas, how they sought to create clarity amidst chaos. Those decisions, preserved through abstraction, continue to guide us. The bridge that abstraction provides is not only between past and future but also between intention and execution. Machines operate in binary, a language alien to human intuition. Through abstraction we bring machine language closer to human thought, allowing ideas to be communicated across the divide. This communication is what allows code to be read, understood, and built upon. Without abstraction, code would remain inaccessible, locked away in the esoteric symbols of the machine. With abstraction, it becomes a living language that connects human intention to machine execution and future interpretation. As we look ahead to the challenges of building systems that must endure in an era of rapid change, the role of abstraction will only grow more vital. Emerging technologies may transform the way machines execute instructions, but abstraction will continue to be the bridge that ensures human ideas are preserved. Whether through new paradigms like functional programming, reactive systems, or even the abstractions of artificial intelligence, the principle remains the same. Abstraction is the tool by which we capture ideas in a form that can outlive us. To embrace abstraction fully is to accept responsibility. Every abstraction chosen carries weight. It decides what will be remembered and what will be forgotten. It determines how easily future generations can interpret our intent. It defines whether our work will vanish from the machines we used or endure as part of a larger intellectual tradition. The invisible architects of continuity are those who wield abstraction with care, with foresight, and with humility. They know that the code they write is temporary, but the abstractions they shape can be eternal. In the end abstraction is the true author of permanence in code. It is the bridge that connects the fleeting with the enduring, the mechanical with the conceptual, the immediate with the timeless. Through abstraction, ephemeral code becomes more than a tool for the present. It becomes part of the living memory of humanity, a record of thought that carries forward into the future. And it is through abstraction that programmers, whether they realize it or not, inscribe their legacy upon the fabric of time.

The Fragility and Strength of Digital Memory

When we think of memory we often think of human recollection, of how stories are passed down orally, of how parchment preserved the words of civilizations, or of how libraries attempted to capture knowledge across generations. Yet digital memory stands apart. It is built on the most fragile of materials, electrons flowing through circuits and magnetic states encoded on surfaces that can be wiped away in an instant. At the same time, it is paradoxically stronger than any memory humankind has ever known, for it can replicate itself endlessly across machines, networks, and continents. The fragility and strength of digital memory coexist in a constant tension, one that shapes the legacy of code and determines whether the work of today will still echo centuries from now. Digital memory is fragile because it depends on the persistence of machines that themselves are temporary. Hard drives degrade, magnetic tapes demagnetize, solid state storage cells leak, and servers are replaced in endless cycles of obsolescence. A simple power surge or a neglected backup policy can erase entire decades of work. Fragility lies also in the fleeting nature of formats and standards. A file written in an obsolete word processor or saved in a once popular compression scheme might be unreadable a few decades later. In this sense memory is fragile not only in its physical substrate but also in its dependence on the tools of interpretation. To read the memory of yesterday requires the language of yesterday, and languages fall out of favor as quickly as hardware is discarded. Yet this fragility is only half the story. Digital memory is also immensely strong because of its ability to replicate and distribute. Once a piece of code or data is released into a global network it can exist in thousands or millions of copies, far beyond the control of its author. Even if a particular machine fails, the idea it contains may survive countless others. Replication gives digital memory a resilience that no single manuscript or carved tablet could ever achieve. Consider the works of ancient philosophers: only fragments survived because only a handful of scrolls were copied and preserved. Now consider a piece of open-source software released today: it may be cloned, mirrored, forked, and backed up across hundreds of platforms within hours of publication. The tension between fragility and strength makes digital memory unique in the history of human knowledge. But to understand the legacy of code we must look deeper into how memory functions not just as storage but as continuity. Every piece of code is both an artifact and an instruction. It is an artifact because it embodies the choices, style, and logic of its author. It is an instruction because it compels a machine to behave in a particular way when executed. Memory therefore is not static. It is dynamic, constantly brought back to life when compiled, interpreted, or run. This duality means that memory in code is never only about what is stored but also about what can be enacted. A manuscript on a shelf remains still until read. Code, once executed, transforms memory into motion, and that is what makes it fragile and strong simultaneously.

Fragility often reveals itself when systems depend on a single line of continuity. Imagine a company that builds its infrastructure on a proprietary platform from the 1990s. If the company fails to migrate, if backups are lost, or if documentation is misplaced, then the entire foundation may collapse when hardware becomes unavailable. The strength of memory comes not from singularity but from redundancy. The Internet Archive has preserved vast amounts of digital history because it insists on creating copies across many servers. Similarly distributed version control systems thrive because every developer carries a complete copy of history. This is resilience born of multiplicity, and it is an antidote to fragility.

Yet even redundancy has limits. The strength of memory must contend with the erosion of meaning. To store is not always to understand. Vast archives of software exist whose operation is opaque because the context in which they were written has been lost. Without documentation, without comments, without cultural or institutional knowledge, memory becomes fossilized.

It remains, but it does not speak. This is where fragility reasserts itself. A line of code might survive for centuries in archives, but if no one knows what it means or how to execute it, then its survival is symbolic rather than practical. The strength of memory depends not only on bits that persist but on the continuity of understanding that surrounds them. One of the most profound challenges in the age of digital legacy is the question of emulation. Hardware evolves rapidly, operating systems rise and fall, and dependencies vanish. If memory is to endure, environments must be recreated. Emulation allows modern machines to simulate the architectures of the past, preserving not just files but the capacity to bring them to life. This shows that memory is not only about what is stored but about how it can be resurrected. Without emulation the fragility of code is overwhelming. With emulation strength emerges because the past remains executable. But emulation too is precarious, for it demands careful design and preservation across generations. Strength is also revealed through the collective will of communities. Open-source projects thrive not simply because of code replication but because of living stewardship. Communities keep memory alive by continuing to document, refine, and build upon what came before. In such spaces memory becomes more than a set of instructions. It becomes a living tradition. Consider the Linux kernel which has evolved over decades. Its strength lies not only in the code but in the culture of contributors who pass on knowledge and sustain its meaning. Memory here is both technical and social, and this dual strength makes it remarkably enduring. The fragility of memory reminds us that digital permanence is not automatic. Unlike stone carvings or clay tablets which endure through physical resilience, digital artifacts demand active care. A line of code not backed up, a repository not mirrored, or a project not documented can vanish more quickly than ink exposed to fire. Fragility humbles us, reminding us that the abundance of digital copies can foster complacency. It is easy to believe that because data is everywhere it is also safe, yet history is filled with stories of lost archives, corrupt disks, and abandoned platforms. Strength without stewardship degenerates into illusion.

We see this paradox most vividly in the fate of early web culture. Many of the websites that defined the dawn of the Internet have disappeared. Their code was not preserved, their media files vanished, and their links decayed. This is digital fragility in its starkest form, a reminder that the strongest medium in history can also become the most perishable. At the same time, we also see strength in projects like the Internet Archive, in the distributed survival of protocols such as email, and in the countless open projects that continue to thrive decades after their inception. The same medium that erases can also preserve in ways that no physical medium could.

If we view code as legacy, we must understand memory not as a guarantee but as a responsibility. Fragility warns us that preservation cannot be left to chance. Strength assures us that with deliberate effort legacy can outlast the author. Architects of continuity must design systems that do not depend on singular points of failure. They must cultivate documentation, redundancy, open standards, and community stewardship. The balance between fragility and strength is not decided by technology alone but by human intent. The ultimate lesson is that memory is not just about data storage but about meaning, accessibility, and continuity. To write code without considering its preservation is to leave behind a message in ink that will fade in the rain. To build with care is to carve into the collective memory of humanity, ensuring that when future generations uncover the code they will not only see instructions but also understand the vision behind them. Fragility and strength coexist, and in that coexistence lies the destiny of digital legacy.

Legacy as a Living Conversation Between Past and Future

Legacy in code is often misunderstood as something fixed and sealed once a project has been completed or a system has been archived. Yet when we look closer at how systems evolve and how ideas within them travel through time, we see that legacy is not a static monument but a conversation that continues long after the original author has stepped away. Each line of code written today speaks not only to the machine that executes it but also to the future programmers, architects, and thinkers who will read, adapt, and reinterpret it. Code becomes the bridge through which voices from the past shape the thinking of those who inherit the responsibility of building tomorrow's systems. This dialogue is not one-directional. Just as the past influences the future, the future reshapes the way the past is understood. The code of yesterday is read through the lens of today's priorities, practices, and possibilities, which means the conversation is dynamic and alive.

The concept of legacy as a living conversation requires us to see systems not merely as technical constructs but as cultural artifacts that evolve as part of a shared intellectual tradition. When a programmer documents their thought process, chooses a particular architecture, or builds an abstraction, they are embedding their worldview into the structure of the code. Those who inherit that code are not passive consumers but active participants in an ongoing dialogue. They must decide whether to extend the original vision, challenge it, or transform it entirely. In this way, legacy is not just preservation. It is participation, where the decisions of one generation of coders become the foundation for debates and innovations of the next. Consider the survival of ancient languages. Latin, though no longer spoken in daily life, continues to influence legal terminology, scientific nomenclature, and religious traditions. Its legacy lives not as a frozen relic but as a living influence that still shapes the way societies frame knowledge. In the same way, code that has outlived its authors continues to shape the intellectual and practical terrain of software. Systems written in languages that are no longer dominant, like Fortran or COBOL, still power industries, institutions, and infrastructures. They are kept alive not merely out of necessity but because they carry a deep conversation between past design choices and present demands. Every developer who touches those systems adds to the story, and in doing so, extends the dialogue into the future.

To understand legacy as a conversation is to recognize that the people who come after us are not only inheritors but also co-authors. They will leave their imprints, their interpretations, and their corrections on the body of work we leave behind. What we call legacy systems are in reality evolving dialogues written in the language of code. This reframing shifts how we think about writing systems today. Instead of assuming that our work will one day be obsolete, we must see it as part of a living lineage. Each function, module, and architecture we design is a statement in an ongoing debate that will continue long after us. The question then is not whether our code will last forever but how we can contribute meaningfully to a conversation that will outlive us. This perspective introduces an ethical dimension to coding. When we know that our work will be inherited, adapted, and reinterpreted, we carry a responsibility to write in ways that invite understanding rather than confusion. Clear documentation, thoughtful abstraction, and ethical considerations become essential because they serve as the voice we project into the future. The developers who come after us will either thank us for clarity or struggle against the opacity we leave behind. In this sense, legacy is not only a technical inheritance but also a moral one. It reflects whether we saw our role as temporary builders or as stewards of a dialogue that spans generations. Legacy as conversation also reveals the tension between permanence and transformation. No matter how carefully a system is designed, it cannot remain untouched. Future developers will add, modify, or even dismantle parts of it. Yet this does not erase the original voice. Instead, it creates layers, much like the palimpsests of ancient manuscripts where new writings were inscribed over older ones, but traces of the original remained. Code, too, becomes a layered text, where past and future voices intermingle. The original author may have intended one thing, but through time the system acquires meanings and functions that even its creator could not have foreseen. There is a humility in recognizing that the systems we build are not final. They are chapters in a larger book that will be written long after us. This humility does not diminish the importance of our contributions. On the contrary, it places them within a lineage of intellectual continuity. Just as a philosopher contributes to a centuries-long discourse on ethics, or a poet adds to the evolving tradition of literature, a programmer contributes to a dialogue that stretches across generations of technical thought. Our work matters because it becomes part of something larger than ourselves, something that grows richer with each new participant.

This understanding of legacy challenges the obsession with novelty that dominates much of modern technology. In a culture that often values disruption over continuity, it is tempting to dismiss the old as irrelevant. Yet when we see code as conversation, we realize that novelty without continuity is like shouting into the void. True innovation emerges when we build upon the voices that came before us, acknowledging their insights and mistakes while adding our own perspective. Legacy becomes the soil from which genuine progress grows. The dialogue between past and future also reveals how fragile legacy can be. Conversations can be lost if the participants stop listening. In code, this happens when documentation is neglected, when systems are abandoned without explanation, or when knowledge is hoarded rather than shared. Silence in such cases does not mean the system ceases to exist. It means the conversation has been broken, leaving future developers to struggle with fragments of a language they no longer fully understand. To ensure continuity, we must not only write code but also cultivate the practices that keep the conversation alive. Examples from history show us both the successes and failures of this continuity. The works of Aristotle, preserved through translations and commentaries, continued to influence Western and Islamic philosophy for centuries. Meanwhile, entire bodies of ancient knowledge, such as the mathematical traditions of the Babylonians, were lost for centuries because they were not preserved in accessible forms. In software, too, we see this duality. Open-source projects thrive when they foster inclusive communities that keep the dialogue alive, while closed systems often wither when they lose their original maintainers. The vitality of a legacy depends not on its technical perfection but on the strength of the conversation it sustains. As coders, architects, and thinkers, our role is not merely to create systems but to ensure that they remain part of this larger dialogue. This requires humility, patience, and vision. It requires us to look beyond the immediate utility of our work and imagine how it might be read by someone decades from now. What assumptions will they find embedded in our code? What values will they detect in the structures we leave behind? Will they see evidence of care, thought, and responsibility, or will they see a disregard for those who would follow? These questions transform coding from a task of execution into an act of legacy building. Ultimately, legacy as a living conversation means that immortality in code is not about permanence of structure but about continuity of dialogue. Just as human ideas survive by being repeated, debated, and reimagined, code survives by being used, understood, and adapted. The true measure of a system's endurance is not whether it remains untouched but whether it remains intelligible, relevant, and capable of sparking new contributions. In this sense, every programmer is not only a builder of systems but also a participant in a centuries-long dialogue about how humans shape the digital world. To see legacy this way is to see ourselves as part of something enduring, where the work of today becomes the voice of tomorrow and where the future is always in conversation with the past.

Chapter Six

Code as the Silent Witness of Human History

When we attempt to measure the span of human civilization we often reach for stone monuments, manuscripts, and oral traditions as vessels of continuity. Yet in the present age a new vessel has emerged that holds its own authority over memory and preservation. That vessel is code. It speaks in silence. It lives in syntax. It listens without ears and remembers without the limitations of human recall. Code becomes the silent witness of human history not because it consciously observes but because it records actions and systems with a fidelity that exceeds parchment or stone. What makes this silence so compelling is that it carries meaning without the need for constant speech. Systems continue running. Logs are written. Functions execute. And through this ongoing quiet repetition history is preserved in a form both mechanical and eternal. One might ask how code qualifies as history when it is not narrative in the traditional sense. The answer lies in how history itself is constructed. Historians rely on records, on marks left by those who lived before us. A receipt for grain in ancient Mesopotamia tells us about commerce just as much as a poem tells us about culture. Likewise a snippet of assembly code from the early days of computing tells us about technological ambition, intellectual methods, and the constraints of the time. It does not need to tell a story through words in order to be historical. Its existence as a fragment of thought translated into machine logic already positions it as a witness to a moment in human imagination.

The silence of code is not absence. It is density. Within a compressed algorithm lies the collective problem solving of its creators. Every function designed to sort numbers or transmit packets encapsulates the urgency of a human need. What we witness in archives of code are silent testimonies of curiosity, urgency, and survival. When the Apollo Guidance Computer code was recovered and studied decades after the moon landings, researchers saw not only the clever engineering required to overcome limited memory but also the persistence of human ambition that could not be contained by the boundary's of 1960s hardware. That code silently carried the memory of reaching beyond Earth itself. To describe code as a silent witness is also to acknowledge its neutrality. Unlike a diary or memoir, it does not embellish. It does not favor one interpretation of an event over another. It executes what is written. It may fail due to error or limitation, but it does not attempt to distort. This quality makes it a unique vessel of continuity because it removes the variability of subjective memory. It can be wrong in design but never deceitful in essence. The wrongness of a flawed algorithm still reveals as much about its time as the success of a perfected one.

Consider the millions of lines of code running in old banking systems across the world. Much of this was written in COBOL, a language now viewed by many as outdated. Yet within that code lies the silent continuity of economies. Transactions have flowed, salaries have been paid, and savings have been recorded across generations. For decades the programmers behind those systems may have retired, passed away, or moved into other fields, but their lines remain active. Those lines silently witness the transfer of wealth, the collapse of markets, and the endurance of institutions. They preserve not just the record of computation but the very rhythm of societies. Silence as continuity emerges most powerfully when code outlives its creators. This is where the metaphor of witness deepens. A witness is often called upon in courts or inquiries to testify about what was seen. Code testifies without speech. It proves through its persistence. When a twenty-year-old script continues to automate a task that would otherwise require endless manual labor, it is testifying to the foresight of its author. It proves that at one point a human imagined efficiency and encoded it so faithfully that it could continue to serve beyond its intended horizon. Yet this silent witnessing is not without fragility. Code must be maintained, translated, or preserved to continue its testimony. Otherwise, silence turns into oblivion. Digital decay, bit rot, and changing platforms can silence code permanently. What makes this particularly striking is that unlike manuscripts or ruins which can survive partially damaged, code often requires complete integrity to remain useful. A single corruption can render a system unusable. Thus, the silence of code as witness is precarious. It is a silence that requires guardians. Archivists, digital historians, and preservationists become stewards of this continuity, ensuring that what was once written can continue to speak silently across time. If we step back and imagine the arc of human history through the lens of code, we begin to see a record unlike any other. From the first punched cards used in Jacquard looms to modern neural networks, we witness humanity's trajectory not only of technological growth but of imagination. Code records our desires to automate, to accelerate, to connect, to create. It does not editorialize. It preserves what we attempted and how we attempted it. In this sense it is a form of collective diary but stripped of adjectives and opinions. It is a diary of mechanisms. The silence of code also shapes the way future generations will interpret us. Just as archaeologists examine pottery shards to reconstruct the life of ancient people, future historians may analyze old repositories to reconstruct the priorities of our time. They may examine social media platform code to understand how we engineered human interaction. They may look at climate simulation programs to grasp how we modeled the earth's fragility. They may study encryption algorithms to uncover how we balanced security with freedom. These investigations will not rely on our words about ourselves but on the silent testimony left behind in systems that once governed daily life.

Silence is often mistaken for emptiness but in the context of code it is potential. Every unexecuted function waits with potential energy, ready to testify once triggered. Every archive that lies dormant on forgotten servers carries the possibility of rediscovery. The silent witness is not dead. It is sleeping. And when awakened it can reveal patterns of thought and practice that we ourselves may have forgotten. In this way code becomes not only the record of history but the mirror that reminds us of paths we once walked.

What deepens the metaphor further is the contrast between noise and silence in digital culture. The world is filled with constant chatter of updates, notifications, and endless streams of content. Yet beneath this noise lies the silent layer of code that sustains it. Without ever demanding recognition these silent layer's structure the rhythm of modern life. The fact that they rarely speak aloud is what grants them their authority. They remain invisible yet absolute, shaping the contours of existence while saying nothing. The silence of code also invites ethical reflection. If code testifies to human history, then what responsibility do we hold as its authors. A flawed algorithm that enforces inequality or misrepresents data will also stand as silent witness to our moral failures. Just as ruins reveal not only the greatness of past empires but also their mistakes, code reveals our blind spots. Its silence does not absolve us. It magnifies. The logs of a discriminatory system will outlast excuses. The binaries of destructive software will outlast apologies. In this way the silent witness is not only a preserver of progress but also a judge of conscience.

It is tempting to view silence as passive, but code proves otherwise. The silence of systems that continue running shapes human behavior actively. Consider how navigation algorithms silently redirect millions of travelers daily. Consider how recommendation systems silently curate what we watch or read. These systems rarely explain themselves in words. They act. And through their silent actions they witness and alter history simultaneously. The witness becomes participant. The silence becomes power. In the broader arc of civilization this role of code as silent witness may be one of the most profound cultural transformations of our era. We are accustomed to seeing human history through artifacts and language, through stories and voices. To now have an enduring witness that operates without voice but with mechanical fidelity changes the nature of historical continuity. It suggests that the future will not only read about us but will also interact with the very mechanisms we left behind. They will not only see records of how we lived but they may run our code to simulate our intentions. The silent witness of code thus exists at multiple layers. At the individual level, it preserves the small efforts of programmers who solved local problems. At the societal level, it carries forward the infrastructure of economies, communication, and governance. At the civilizational level, it preserves the reach of human imagination. Across these layers the silence remains constant. Code does not shout. It persists. It does not boast. It endures. In conclusion, to speak of code as the silent witness of human history is to acknowledge a profound truth. We are the only species to create languages that machines can execute, and in those executions lies a continuity that transcends our lifespans. Code remembers us without words. It carries forward our successes and failures with equal fidelity. It stands silently at the edge of time, witnessing without interruption, recording without judgment, and waiting to be rediscovered by those who will come after us. It is the voice we will never hear but the testimony that will never vanish.

The Tension Between Obsolescence and Immortality

Code lives in the paradox of being both destined to vanish and determined to endure. Every line is written under the shadow of technological obsolescence, for languages evolve, paradigms shift, platforms rise and collapse, and what is useful today may be incomprehensible tomorrow. Yet at the same time, code aspires to immortality, for embedded within it are human attempts to fix logic into eternity, to etch solutions into a medium that might outlive the very world that inspired them. This duality makes software not merely a tool but a living archive of human ambition, carrying in its fragile syntax the struggle between decay and endurance. To understand this tension, one must first see how quickly obsolescence arrives in the digital world. A system written only two decades ago may already be incompatible with modern compilers, operating systems, or hardware architectures. The code itself may remain intact, its logic preserved line by line, but the ecosystem it depends on could have dissolved, leaving the once functional script stranded in silence. Programmers describe this as bit rot or software erosion, yet the more accurate description is cultural dislocation. Code does not die because it ceases to have meaning; it dies because the culture of its interpretation vanishes. Without compilers, interpreters, and communities that breathe life into its patterns, it becomes inert text, fossilized yet unreachable. However, immortality creeps in through preservation, emulation, and the relentless need for continuity. Consider the persistence of COBOL in the infrastructure of global finance. Despite being conceived in an era of punch cards and mainframes, its presence endures, silently orchestrating billions of transactions daily. It exists as proof that some systems refuse to vanish, even when the world forgets how to read them fully. The persistence of such languages demonstrates that obsolescence is never absolute; it is negotiated by necessity, relevance, and the cost of abandonment.

The tension grows sharper when one looks at systems designed with planned obsolescence. Modern development environments encourage rapid iteration, discarding older frameworks for newer ones with better abstractions. This cycle accelerates obsolescence intentionally, often in the name of efficiency, security, or innovation. Yet every discarded framework contains a story, an approach to solving problems, an intellectual footprint that, though abandoned in practice, remains meaningful in history. Here lies the paradox: by discarding old systems, we seem to accelerate death, yet by documenting and archiving them, we paradoxically grant them immortality as historical artifacts. Immortality also asserts itself in unexpected ways through migration. When a legacy system must be replaced, engineers often translate its logic into a new environment, preserving the essence of the original code in altered form. This translation does not eliminate obsolescence but transforms it into continuity. The original code may no longer run, but its soul persists in the rewritten system, a reincarnation that demonstrates how ideas transcend the syntax that once carried them. In this sense, code does not vanish but evolves, and every translation is an act of resurrection. The conflict between obsolescence and immortality is also a matter of human memory. Developers leave behind fragments of their work in repositories, forums, and archives. Future generations may rediscover these fragments, not as functional tools, but as intellectual artifacts. A snippet of assembly code from the early era of computing might serve no practical purpose today, yet it reveals the creativity and constraint that defined its era. Thus, code that is obsolete in function becomes immortal in meaning. It ceases to be a tool and becomes testimony, carrying forward the ingenuity of those who dared to shape logic in the language of machines.

One cannot ignore the emotional weight of this paradox. Programmers often experience grief when their code becomes obsolete, especially if it once powered systems that were vital to communities or industries. Yet there is also pride in knowing that traces of their work will persist in archives or rewritten descendants. In the digital realm, death is never absolute. The fragments remain, scattered across repositories, embedded in other systems, or preserved in the collective memory of developers. This lingering presence gives code a ghostly immortality, haunting new generations with whispers of the old. Consider the example of early internet protocols, many of which have been replaced or refined beyond recognition. Though obsolete in practical use, they remain immortal in influence, for every modern standard built upon their foundations. Their specific implementations may no longer function, but the ideas they crystallized still govern the flow of information across the globe. In this way, obsolescence is merely a mask; beneath it, immortality endures. The tension also appears in cultural discussions of digital heritage. As societies recognize the need to preserve digital artifacts, institutions are emerging to archive code with the same reverence given to literature or art. The act of preserving code transforms it from transient tool into cultural legacy. This recognition acknowledges that even when code ceases to run, it holds value as a mirror of the intellectual climate that produced it. Obsolescence strips it of utility, but immortality grants it a place in memory. The paradox stretches further when viewed in terms of language evolution. Just as spoken languages evolve and obsolete dialects linger in archives or influence later forms, programming languages undergo cycles of death and rebirth. A once dominant language may decline into obscurity, yet fragments of its syntax and design resurface in successors. Thus, no language truly vanishes; each leaves traces in the DNA of future systems. Even the most obsolete syntax may echo faintly in modern paradigms, ensuring immortality through influence if not through survival.

The tension is therefore not a problem to solve but a reality to embrace. Obsolescence reminds us of the fragility of our creations, the impermanence of platforms, and the relentless

march of time. Immortality reassures us that nothing truly vanishes, that every system leaves behind fragments of thought, echoes of creativity, and seeds of continuity. Together they form the dual rhythm of the digital cosmos, where every line of code is both fading and enduring at once. In this paradox lies the truth of legacy. Code does not live forever, nor does it die completely. It inhabits the space between obsolescence and immortality, carrying forward fragments of its creators into a future that will reinterpret, transform, and preserve them in ways unimaginable. To write code, then, is to enter into this tension knowingly, crafting not only for the present utility but for the echoes that will persist long after the system has ceased to run.

The Future Written in Invisible Lines

The future of software is not measured only by the lines that compile into an application but by the invisible logic that outlives the present generation of creators. A line of code is more than syntax; it is a reflection of a mind arranging thought into precise order. Yet the deeper power of code lies not in what is visible to compilers or interpreters but in the invisible frameworks, abstractions, and patterns that survive long after the visible has changed. Every language that rises to prominence eventually gives way to another, but within each there are invisible lines that endure, shaping how the next language is written. When one examines the movement from assembly to structured programming, from procedural languages to object orientation, from objects to functional purity and concurrency, the visible expression has shifted dramatically, but the invisible ideas that govern modularity, encapsulation, abstraction, and state remain constant. These invisible lines are not tied to the characters that make up the code but to the architecture of thought embedded within it. They are unseen but indispensable, and they ensure that systems continue to evolve while carrying their past within them. The invisible lines are most evident when one looks at systems that seem disconnected from modern development yet continue to run the world. Banking infrastructure still depends on COBOL, aviation still depends on Ada, manufacturing still depends on PLCs, and operating systems still depend on principles laid down in the 1970s. While new frameworks appear every year with promises of simplicity, efficiency, or speed, these promises rarely to touch the deep invisible lines that stabilize the digital ecosystem. What matters is not whether a function is written with curly braces or indentation, but whether the structure supports reliability, predictability, and adaptability. These are the invisible values encoded in the earliest systems and passed forward, generation after generation. The future is therefore not just about writing new lines but about carrying forward the invisible inheritance embedded in existing ones.

When developers speak of clean architecture or elegant design, they are pointing to invisible qualities that cannot be measured by line count or surface syntax. Scalability is invisible until tested by millions of users. Security is invisible until a vulnerability is exploited. Maintainability is invisible until a new generation of engineers must adapt the system without tearing it apart. These qualities exist not in the code itself but in the unseen choices, in the silent agreements between engineers who may never meet each other. A comment in code is visible, but the decision to reduce coupling or to separate concerns is invisible yet far more consequential. Future generations do not inherit comments; they inherit architecture. To understand the future written in invisible lines, one must recognize that software is not a product, but a living organism shaped by constant mutation. The invisible lines guide its DNA, ensuring that even when languages and platforms evolve, the essential structure survives. In distributed computing, the invisible lines show themselves in consensus protocols, in fault tolerance models, and in the balance between availability and consistency. In artificial intelligence, the invisible lines emerge in probabilistic reasoning, in feedback loops, and in learning models that adjust to new data. These structures cannot be seen by glancing at code files, yet they determine how the system behaves across decades. The future of software will therefore belong to those who can read not only the visible code but also the invisible grammar of systems. The invisible lines also determine the ethics of systems. In a world where algorithms govern financial markets, medical diagnoses, and social interactions, the invisible assumptions embedded in these algorithms become lines that shape human lives. If bias is present, it is rarely visible in explicit conditionals; it exists in training data, in feature selection, in the thresholds chosen for classification. These are invisible decisions that cannot be reviewed by looking at surface code but that direct the behavior of entire societies. The future written in invisible lines therefore requires vigilance, for systems that outlive their creators may carry forward silent prejudices or inequities unless they are confronted and corrected. The power of invisible lines is that they continue acting long after their originators are gone, which is both a gift and a danger. It is important to recognize that invisible lines are not mystical abstractions, but concrete patterns passed forward. Consider the Model-View-Controller paradigm. It began as an experiment in graphical interfaces but became an invisible framework shaping web applications, mobile development, and beyond. Even developers unaware of its origin reproduce its structure because it has become embedded in the cultural DNA of programming. The same is true for relational databases. The idea of tables, joins, and normalization may be expressed through different tools today, but the invisible logic remains dominant. The visible may evolve from SQL to NoSQL and back toward hybrid models, but the invisible demand for structured relationships never disappears. The invisible lines are resilient because they are not dependent on any particular syntax or implementation but on deep human needs: to organize, to predict, to simplify, and to control complexity. As technology moves toward quantum computing, edge systems, and neural architectures, one might imagine a complete break from past structures. Yet even here the invisible lines carry forward. Quantum computing introduces new gates and probabilistic states, but the invisible need for abstraction, error correction, and scalability remains the same. Edge computing disperses computation across billions of devices, but the invisible concern for latency, coordination, and failure recovery persists. Neural architectures transform inputs into layers of representations, but the invisible demand for interpretability, accountability, and reproducibility continues to shape their design. The future written in invisible lines is thus not a discontinuity but a continuity, a long river whose surface currents may change direction while the deep flow remains constant.

One must also consider that invisible lines do not only live within machines but within communities. The unwritten rules of open-source collaboration, the etiquette of code review, the norms of documentation, and the ethics of contribution are all invisible structures that guide the sustainability of projects. A repository may contain thousands of visible lines, but what keeps it alive is the invisible commitment of contributors, the unwritten respect between maintainers, and the silent trust between users and developers. When a project succeeds across decades, it is rarely because of superior syntax but because of these invisible human agreements. The future of code will therefore depend on whether such invisible lines of collaboration remain strong, for without them even the most sophisticated system decays. Finally, the invisible lines remind us that code is not only about efficiency but about meaning. Every system that endures is a dialogue between the past and the future. It is a message sent forward through time, written in invisible ink that only future interpreters can read. The choices we make today are not neutral; they will ripple into environments we cannot imagine. A function written for a local application may one day underpin a global network. A protocol designed for a small-scale experiment may become the foundation of a planetary system. The invisible lines transform every keystroke into an act of legacy. The future will not remember the surface syntax we argue about today, but it will inherit the invisible architecture of our choices.

To write systems that outlive their creators is therefore to understand that permanence does not reside in the visible but in the invisible. The visible is always at risk of obsolescence, but the invisible endures. This truth elevates the responsibility of programmers beyond technical competence toward historical awareness. They are not merely solving present problems; they are inscribing invisible lines into the memory of civilization. The systems that run tomorrow will do so not because of the beauty

of their syntax but because of the resilience of their invisible design. The future, though unwritten in our present code, is already encoded in these invisible structures, waiting to reveal themselves across time.

Chapter Seven

Foundations of Enduring Systems Designing Software That Lasts

Code becomes a legacy not by existing in the present but by remaining relevant long after its creators have moved on. The first principle of enduring software is architecture designed for longevity. Sustainable systems are modular, logically organized, and resilient to change. Each component is designed to function independently, yet coherently within the larger system. The separation of concerns ensures that modifications in one area do not ripple unpredictably throughout the system. Decisions regarding programming paradigms, frameworks, and libraries are made with foresight, anticipating technological shifts and evolving requirements. Readability, consistency, and clarity are not cosmetic but foundational, enabling future developers to understand intent, trace functionality, and safely extend the system.

Documentation is the connective tissue that preserves knowledge. Code without context is fragile. Comprehensive documentation captures architectural rationale, usage examples, and anticipated modifications. Naming conventions, structured comments, and clear abstractions reduce cognitive load, allowing new contributors to focus on problem-solving rather than deciphering design intent. Systems built with this level of foresight avoid the pitfalls of obsolescence caused by confusion or misinterpretation. Performance considerations are woven into design decisions, ensuring scalability, reliability, and efficiency under changing conditions. Security, stability, and maintainability are not afterthoughts but integral to every architectural choice. Enduring systems anticipate the pressures of time and usage, creating structures that function reliably across years and even decades. Testing frameworks and continuous integration practices further reinforce the longevity of software. By automating validation and ensuring that components behave predictably under evolving circumstances, developers create a safety net that preserves functionality. This proactive approach minimizes the risk of regression and maintains trust in the system. Systems designed to endure balance immediate functionality with strategic foresight. Each line of code is written with consideration for its long-term implications, creating a foundation that future teams can build upon confidently.

Ethical and Societal Dimensions of Legacy Code

Software carries consequences that extend far beyond its creators. Ethical considerations are critical in designing systems that endure responsibly. Decisions about data collection, storage, sharing, and access influence users long after deployment. Privacy, security, and accessibility are not abstract ideals, but practical obligations embedded in sustainable systems. Developers who write code with longevity in mind consider the societal impact of every algorithm, interface, and interaction. Ethical foresight ensures that software supports users equitably and avoids perpetuating harm, bias, or exclusion. Systems created without these considerations risk creating burdens for future maintainers and negative consequences for end users.

Maintainability is inseparable from ethics. Code that is opaque, convoluted, or inconsistent imposes unnecessary difficulty on those who inherit it. Ethical developers prioritize clarity, structure, and documentation to prevent accidental misuse and reduce the likelihood of errors. Transparency in coding practices establishes trust with both internal teams and external stakeholders. Inclusivity is an essential dimension of ethical legacy code. Designing systems accessible to diverse users, adaptable to evolving standards, and resilient to bias ensures relevance and equity. Ethical considerations reinforce both the functional and moral longevity of software, enabling future teams to continue development with confidence and integrity. Security is another ethical imperative. Systems designed to endure must anticipate vulnerabilities that could emerge years after initial deployment. Authentication protocols, encryption practices, and defensive programming techniques preserve trust over time. By integrating ethical principles into design, developers create software that does not merely perform tasks but contributes positively to organizational objectives and societal expectations. Ethical software ensures that legacy is not just technical but principled, leaving a framework that future generations of developers and users can rely upon.

Collaboration, Knowledge Transfer, and Cultural Continuity in Software Legacy

Code achieves true legacy when it transcends individual authorship. Collaboration and knowledge transfer ensure that systems survive personnel changes, organizational shifts, and technological evolution. Teams cultivate continuity through mentorship, code reviews, and shared standards. This culture of care embeds understanding into the organization rather than relying solely on the memory of a few contributors. Each developer participates in creating a living artifact that carries knowledge, methodology, and design philosophy forward. Future contributors inherit not only functional code but the principles, processes, and reasoning that shaped it. Version control, continuous integration, and modular testing preserve history and provide context for evolution. Every change is documented, justified, and reversible, allowing experimentation without compromising stability. These systems create a narrative of development that supports decision-making and safeguards knowledge. Collaboration ensures that insights are disseminated and that collective intelligence guides system evolution. Legacy is reinforced when knowledge is institutionalized rather than siloed, creating a resilient framework capable of adapting to new challenges while honoring the original intent. Cultural continuity is equally essential. Clear coding standards, shared practices, and open communication foster an environment in which knowledge and responsibility are distributed. Developers internalize the philosophy of maintainability, ethical design, and adaptability. This culture ensures that innovation continues without sacrificing coherence or stability. When software is treated as an inheritance rather than a temporary tool, every contributor understands the responsibility of stewardship. Collaboration and culture transform individual effort into enduring organizational capability, enabling systems to outlive their creators while remaining relevant, secure, and functional.

Chapter Eight

Designing for Longevity: Principles of Maintainable and Scalable Systems

Sustainable software is designed to remain functional, adaptable, and valuable over time. Longevity begins with architecture that anticipates change, accommodates growth, and allows modification without disruption. Modular design ensures components can evolve independently, reducing interdependency and complexity. Clear separation of concerns prevents small changes from cascading into unforeseen issues. Developers consider maintainability at every stage, writing code that is consistent, readable, and logically organized. Every function, class, and module is crafted with an awareness that it will be interpreted, extended, or corrected by future developers who may not share the original context or assumptions.

Documentation transforms code from a temporary tool into a durable artifact. Annotations, explanations of design rationale, and practical examples provide future maintainers with context that preserves intent and reduces risk. Documentation complements naming conventions, coding standards, and consistent formatting to create systems that communicate their structure and logic inherently. Well-structured code allows newcomers to understand system behavior quickly, reducing onboarding time and minimizing errors during development. The combination of readable code and comprehensive documentation ensures that the software is self-explanatory, minimizing dependency on human memory or the presence of original creators. Scalability and performance considerations are integral to enduring systems. Systems must handle increased data volume, user demand, and integrations without structural degradation. Anticipating future load and potential bottlenecks allows developers to design systems that remain responsive and efficient. Security is a core component of longevity, protecting data integrity, preserving trust, and safeguarding against vulnerabilities that may emerge as the system grows. The decisions made during development determine whether a system remains viable or becomes obsolete as technology evolves. Software longevity requires balancing immediate needs with strategic foresight, ensuring systems endure through technological shifts, changing business requirements, and evolving user expectations. Testing frameworks, automated validation, and continuous integration enforce reliability and maintainability. By systematically verifying that each component functions as intended, developers create a safety net that preserves functionality over time. Automated testing catches regressions, ensures compatibility, and supports incremental development without compromising stability. By embedding these practices into workflows, organizations institutionalize quality, enabling the software to adapt without collapsing under the weight of complexity. The design of maintainable, scalable, and secure systems is a deliberate practice that transforms transient code into enduring infrastructure, forming the foundation for software that outlives its creators.

Ethical Stewardship and Responsibility in Long-Term Systems

Legacy code carries responsibility far beyond functionality. Ethical stewardship guides developers in designing systems that serve users equitably, protect privacy, and operate securely over time. Decisions regarding data storage, access, and sharing have consequences that extend for years. Developers who embed ethical principles in their work create systems that honor user trust, maintain compliance, and minimize harm. Systems that fail to consider ethics impose burdens on future maintainers, expose organizations to liability, and risk undermining societal norms. Ethical design ensures software contributes positively to users and organizations alike, reinforcing both moral and functional longevity. Maintainability is an ethical concern because opaque, inconsistent, or poorly documented code creates unnecessary friction for those who inherit it. By prioritizing clarity, structure, and accessibility, developers ensure that future contributors can safely extend and improve the system. Transparency in coding practices fosters trust within the organization and among users. Inclusivity is central to ethical legacy code. Systems that accommodate diverse users, follow accessibility standards, and anticipate evolving requirements remain relevant and trusted over time. Ethical principles guide design choices, protecting not only users but the integrity of the software itself, ensuring it remains a reliable and positive tool for those who maintain, use, and depend on it. Security is inseparable from ethical responsibility. Systems must anticipate potential vulnerabilities, implement protective measures, and adapt to emerging threats. Authentication, encryption, and defensive programming preserve data integrity and system trustworthiness. Ethical developers think beyond immediate deadlines, considering the long-term impact of design choices. Systems that balance functionality with security, privacy, and inclusivity endure as trusted artifacts. Ethical stewardship ensures that legacy software is both technically resilient and morally responsible, leaving a framework that future developers can confidently inherit and extend.

Knowledge Transfer and Organizational Continuity

Code transcends its creators when knowledge is effectively shared and preserved. Organizational continuity is achieved through structured collaboration, mentorship, and documentation practices. Systems survive personnel changes, reorganizations, and evolving technologies when teams maintain a shared understanding of architecture, design rationale, and operational practices. Legacy is not built on individual brilliance alone but on processes that embed insight into the organization. Every contributor participates in cultivating understanding, ensuring that knowledge is codified rather than residing solely in memory. Version control, modular testing, and automated workflows preserve history and provide context for evolution. Every modification is tracked, justified, and reversible, allowing experimentation without risking stability. These practices institutionalize knowledge, making the system resilient to turnover and adaptation over time. Culture reinforces this continuity. Teams adhere to shared coding standards, communicate openly, and collaborate consistently. New contributors inherit both the code and the mindset required to maintain, extend, and evolve it responsibly. Adaptability within teams is essential for sustaining software legacy. Structured onboarding, cross-functional communication, and transparent decision-making ensure that future developers can understand and modify the system without disrupting its integrity. Collaborative practices transform individual effort into collective legacy, enabling systems to remain functional, relevant, and secure long after the original developers have departed. Knowledge transfer, coupled with cultural continuity, ensures that software is treated as an inheritance, not a transient artifact.

The combination of documented rationale, shared practices, and collaborative stewardship preserves the system's purpose, integrity, and adaptability for generations of developers to come.

Chapter Nine

The Enduring Organizational Impact of Legacy Code

Software does more than automate processes; it becomes an enduring pillar of organizational structure. Legacy code shapes workflows, informs strategic decisions, and influences cultural norms within the companies that adopt it. Systems created with foresight guide behavior, define operational boundaries, and enable efficiency in ways that persist long after the original developers have departed. Decisions made during development propagate into the future, creating standards and practices that influence how teams collaborate, how managers prioritize projects, and how resources are allocated. Every architectural choice carries long-term organizational consequences. Well-designed software embeds processes into its architecture. Automated workflows, data validation, and system constraints codify best practices, ensuring consistency across departments. Teams follow the rules and patterns established in the code, not simply because of policy but because the system itself enforces efficiency and accuracy. Legacy systems institutionalize knowledge, reducing reliance on human memory and minimizing errors that could disrupt operations. This enduring influence creates a framework within which organizations operate, allowing for growth and adaptation without losing coherence or stability.

Integration with existing processes amplifies this impact. Systems that are modular, well-documented, and scalable become the foundation for subsequent innovation. They serve as templates for future development, guiding teams in building new functionality aligned with the original vision. Legacy code therefore shapes both the present and future capabilities of the organization, creating a continuous thread of influence that extends far beyond the initial implementation. The cultural impact is equally significant. Systems that prioritize transparency, maintainability, and ethical practices establish norms within teams. Developers and users internalize these standards, influencing how they approach problem-solving, collaboration, and decision-making. By embedding thoughtful design into the codebase, organizations cultivate a culture of discipline, foresight, and responsibility that endures across generations of employees.

Societal Influence and the Broad Reach of Code

Beyond organizational boundaries, software has the power to shape society. Systems designed for longevity influence how people interact with technology, access information, and engage with services. Platforms, applications, and algorithms establish standards that become normalized in public behavior and expectation. Decisions about data privacy, user interface design, and accessibility affect countless individuals over time, creating a social impact that outlasts the creators. Responsible software design considers these implications, recognizing that the system's reach extends into communities, industries, and even public policy. Legacy code can amplify ethical or harmful practices depending on design choices. Algorithms that perpetuate bias or inaccessible interfaces create barriers that persist, affecting users long after deployment. Conversely, systems built with inclusivity, transparency, and ethical principles promote trust, equity, and empowerment. Developers who write for longevity consider the consequences of each function, interaction, and data collection practice. They understand that software serves as a long-term agent of influence, shaping norms, expectations, and behaviors in ways that extend far beyond its immediate context. The societal impact also encompasses innovation adoption. Legacy systems establish patterns that guide industry standards, inform regulatory frameworks, and influence competitor behavior. When systems are widely used, their architecture, assumptions, and workflows propagate across the market, creating implicit norms. Future developers, businesses, and users inherit these patterns, often adopting them as default practices. This propagation magnifies the influence of thoughtful design and ethical coding, extending its reach across industries and communities.

Ultimately, software becomes a vehicle for legacy in society, embedding values, operational principles, and ethical considerations into the fabric of collective experience. Systems outlive their creators because they continue to influence how organizations operate, how industries evolve, and how individuals engage with technology and information. Developers who embrace this perspective write with responsibility, foresight, and an awareness that their work is a contribution to society's ongoing technological and cultural narrative.

Preserving and Evolving Software for Future Generations

The final dimension of legacy code lies in its preservation and evolution. Systems must be maintained, adapted, and extended to remain relevant in changing technological and social landscapes. Practices that ensure continuity include version control, modularity, automated testing, and comprehensive documentation. These mechanisms capture history, track decisions, and provide guidance for future contributors. When maintained effectively, software becomes a durable infrastructure, capable of evolving without losing coherence or intent.

Knowledge transfer is critical to sustaining software. Onboarding, mentoring, and collaborative practices embed understanding into the organization. New developers inherit both the code and the philosophy that shaped it. This continuity ensures that systems can adapt to emerging requirements, integrate new technologies, and remain secure and efficient over time. Legacy software is not static; it is a living artifact that evolves in response to changing needs while preserving its core principles. Adaptation requires foresight. Developers anticipate future use cases, potential integrations, and technological shifts. They design systems to be flexible, supporting extension without compromise. Cultural continuity reinforces this adaptability, ensuring that teams internalize values of maintainability, ethical responsibility, and operational discipline. Legacy software becomes a framework for future innovation, enabling organizations to evolve while preserving the lessons, standards, and principles embedded in the original design. Ultimately, software that achieves true legacy shapes organizations, society, and technological ecosystems across generations. By designing with foresight, maintaining ethical standards, embedding knowledge into organizational culture, and facilitating evolution, developers create systems that endure. Code becomes more than functional artifacts; it is a conduit for influence, a reflection of values, and a tool for perpetual relevance. Legacy software outlives its creators not because of lines of code alone but because of the principles, practices, and foresight embedded within it.

Chapter Ten

The Philosophy of Enduring Code Designing with Legacy in Mind

Legacy code is a product of intentionality. It does not merely serve immediate functionality but reflects foresight, ethical responsibility, and strategic thinking. Creating software with longevity requires a mindset that anticipates the future of the system, its maintainers, and its users. Developers must approach design not as temporary problem-solving but as crafting infrastructure that carries knowledge, operational principles, and societal influence forward. Every choice, from algorithm selection to data handling, from modular design to naming conventions, contributes to a legacy that will shape the organization and its ecosystem for years to come. At the philosophical core of enduring code is the recognition that software is both functional and cultural. Each system embeds norms, processes, and values. Well-designed code communicates intent, enforces best practices, and institutionalizes organizational knowledge. Developers writing for longevity embrace clarity, maintainability, and flexibility as guiding principles. Modular structures enable evolution without collapse, while robust testing ensures that integrity is preserved even as changes accumulate. Documentation, internal guidelines, and code reviews reinforce the philosophy, transforming tacit knowledge into tangible inheritance. A system designed for endurance also anticipates external pressures. Scalability, integration, and security are not merely technical challenges but aspects of longevity philosophy. Systems must accommodate growth, remain resilient to evolving user behavior, and adapt to technological shifts. Security is a moral as well as functional concern. Protecting data, preventing breaches, and safeguarding user trust ensures the system remains reliable and respected over time. Ethical foresight extends beyond immediate compliance; it ensures that software continues to serve its intended purpose responsibly, influencing users, organizations, and communities positively long after its original creators are gone.

Philosophical commitment to longevity also entails embracing change. Code that is rigid or brittle becomes obsolete, no matter how well-written initially. Developers anticipate evolution and design systems that can grow and transform. This involves anticipating modularity needs, designing interfaces that accommodate future expansion, and establishing standards that balance consistency with adaptability. Legacy code is therefore a living philosophy embodied in functional architecture, ethical practice, and cultural foresight. Every line of code, every decision, every principle contributes to a system that outlives the creator while preserving purpose, integrity, and utility.

Systems of Knowledge Transfer: Preserving Understanding Across Generations

Code achieves its fullest impact when understanding and expertise are propagated alongside the software itself. Knowledge transfer is central to ensuring that systems remain functional, maintainable, and relevant across time. Structured documentation, code annotations, architectural diagrams, and design rationales create a map for future developers. These artifacts capture not just how the system works but why it was designed in a particular way. By preserving reasoning alongside functionality, knowledge transfer prevents the dilution of purpose and mitigates risks of misinterpretation or accidental regression. Mentorship and collaborative practices reinforce knowledge continuity. Senior developers guide newcomers, contextualizing design decisions, explaining system patterns, and embedding organizational culture into technical practices. Code reviews, pair programming, and cross-team collaboration provide opportunities to internalize standards and philosophies that are not always explicit in documentation. Knowledge is institutionalized rather than residing in individual memory, transforming the software into a vessel for collective understanding. Version control, modular testing, and continuous integration form the operational backbone of knowledge preservation. Every change is tracked, tested, and documented. These mechanisms ensure that modifications are reversible, traceable, and transparent. They provide a historical narrative of the system, allowing future developers to understand the evolution of the code, identify patterns, and make informed decisions. Modular architectures further enhance knowledge propagation by encapsulating functionality, clarifying dependencies, and simplifying comprehension. Cultural continuity complements technical knowledge transfer. Teams that embrace shared coding standards, open communication, and collaborative problem-solving ensure that principles, practices, and operational understanding persist. New contributors inherit not only the code, but the philosophy and methodology embedded in it. When knowledge is preserved systematically, software becomes a living legacy, capable of evolving while retaining coherence, purpose, and utility. Legacy code therefore embodies both functional systems and the intellectual inheritance necessary for perpetual relevance.

Sustaining Purpose and Influence Through Adaptation

The final dimension of software legacy lies in adaptation. Systems must remain relevant and effective in the face of technological evolution, changing user behavior, and shifting organizational needs. Adaptation requires foresight, modularity, and cultural continuity. Developers anticipate emerging requirements, evolving standards, and future integrations, designing code that can accommodate change without sacrificing integrity. Legacy software is not static; it is a living entity that evolves alongside its environment while preserving foundational purpose. Sustainable systems maintain influence by embedding flexibility in architecture. Interfaces are modular and extensible, allowing future developers to expand capabilities, integrate new technologies, and respond to user needs. Automated testing and validation frameworks ensure stability; while monitoring and analytics provide feedback for informed adaptation. Scalability ensures that systems continue to perform under growing demands. Adaptation preserves both functionality and relevance, allowing software to remain a core tool within organizations and communities.

Purpose is preserved when software remains aligned with organizational objectives and user needs. Systems designed with foresight evolve alongside strategic priorities, integrating new features, adjusting workflows, and maintaining ethical standards. Cultural practices, including continuous learning, mentorship, and collaborative problem-solving, support this evolution by embedding values, standards, and methodologies into the organization. Ethical stewardship ensures that software continues to serve users responsibly, maintaining trust and minimizing risk over time. The influence of legacy software extends beyond functionality. Systems shape organizational behavior, set industry standards, and influence societal norms. Thoughtful design amplifies this influence by embedding principles, processes, and ethical considerations into the architecture. Future developers inherit not just code but the responsibility to sustain its purpose, integrity, and positive impact. Legacy software is therefore a conduit for enduring influence, a testament to foresight, and a framework for perpetual relevance. In conclusion, software legacy is created through philosophy, knowledge transfer, and purposeful adaptation. Developers who write with foresight preserve understanding, and design for evolution ensure that their systems outlive them. Code becomes more than functionality; it is an enduring artifact that shapes organizations, informs future practice, and influences society. Legacy software carries principles forward, sustaining utility, ethical responsibility, and relevance across generations, leaving a mark that transcends its creators.

www.ingramcontent.com/pod-product-compliance
Lightning Source LLC
Chambersburg PA
CBHW021215250926
51852CB00006B/17
* 9 7 8 4 6 9 2 7 7 9 2 1 5 *